T0194774

Published by Macat International Ltd
24:13 Coda Centre, 189 Munster Road, London SW6 6AW.

Distributed exclusively by Routledge
2 Park Square, Milton Park, Abingdon, Oxon OX14 4RN
711 Third Avenue, New York, NY 10017, USA

Routledge is an imprint of the Taylor & Francis Group, an informa business

www.macat.com
info@macat.com

Cataloguing in Publication Data
A catalogue record for this book is available from the British Library.
Library of Congress Cataloguing-in-Publication Data is available upon request.
Cover illustration: Etienne Gilfillan

ISBN 978-1-912302-24-6 (hardback)
ISBN 978-1-912127-59-7 (paperback)
ISBN 978-1-912281-12-1 (e-book)

Notice
The information in this book is designed to orientate readers of the work under analysis,
to elucidate and contextualise its key ideas and themes, and to aid in the development
of critical thinking skills. It is not meant to be used, nor should it be used, as a
substitute for original thinking or in place of original writing or research. References and
notes are provided for informational purposes and their presence does not constitute
endorsement of the information or opinions therein. This book is presented solely for
educational purposes. It is sold on the understanding that the publisher is not engaged
to provide any scholarly advice. The publisher has made every effort to ensure that
this book is accurate and up-to-date, but makes no warranties or representations with
regard to the completeness or reliability of the information it contains. The information
and the opinions provided herein are not guaranteed or warranted to produce particular
results and may not be suitable for students of every ability. The publisher shall not be
liable for any loss, damage or disruption arising from any errors or omissions, or from
the use of this book, including, but not limited to, special, incidental, consequential or
other damages caused, or alleged to have been caused, directly or indirectly, by the
information contained within.

An Analysis of

Friedrich Hayek's
The Road to Serfdom

David Linden
with
Nick Broten

CONTENTS

THE MACAT LIBRARY

The Macat Library is a series of unique academic explorations of seminal works in the humanities and social sciences – books and papers that have had a significant and widely recognised impact on their disciplines. It has been created to serve as much more than just a summary of what lies between the covers of a great book. It illuminates and explores the influences on, ideas of, and impact of that book. Our goal is to offer a learning resource that encourages critical thinking and fosters a better, deeper understanding of important ideas.

Each publication is divided into three Sections: Influences, Ideas, and Impact. Each Section has four Modules. These explore every important facet of the work, and the responses to it.

This Section-Module structure makes a Macat Library book easy to use, but it has another important feature. Because each Macat book is written to the same format, it is possible (and encouraged!) to cross-reference multiple Macat books along the same lines of inquiry or research. This allows the reader to open up interesting interdisciplinary pathways.

To further aid your reading, lists of glossary terms and people mentioned are included at the end of this book (these are indicated by an asterisk [*] throughout) – as well as a list of works cited.

Macat has worked with the University of Cambridge to identify the elements of critical thinking and understand the ways in which six different skills combine to enable effective thinking.
Three allow us to fully understand a problem; three more give us the tools to solve it. Together, these six skills make up the **PACIER** model of critical thinking. They are:

ANALYSIS – understanding how an argument is built
EVALUATION – exploring the strengths and weaknesses of an argument
INTERPRETATION – understanding issues of meaning

CREATIVE THINKING – coming up with new ideas and fresh connections
PROBLEM-SOLVING – producing strong solutions
REASONING – creating strong arguments

To find out more, visit **WWW.MACAT.COM.**

CRITICAL THINKING AND *THE ROAD TO SERFDOM*

Primary critical thinking skill: REASONING
Secondary critical thinking skill: EVALUATION

Friedrich Hayek's 1944 *The Road to Serfdom* is a classic of conservative economic argument. While undeniably a product of a specific time in global politics – which saw the threat of fascism from Nazi Germany and its allies beguilingly answered by the promises of socialism – Hayek's carefully constructed argument is a fine example of the importance of good reasoning in critical thinking.

Reasoning is the art of constructing good, persuasive arguments by organizing one's thoughts, supporting one's conclusions, and considering counter-arguments along the way. *The Road to Serfdom* illustrates all these skills in action; Hayek's argument was that, while many assumed socialism to be the answer to totalitarian, fascist regimes, the opposite was true. Socialist government's reliance on a large state, centralised control, and bureaucratic planning – he insisted – actually amounts to a different kind of totalitarianism.

Freedom of choice, Hayek continued, is a central requirement of individual freedom, and hence a centrally planned economy inevitably constrains freedom. Though many commentators have sought to counter Hayek's arguments, his reasoning skills won over many of the politicians who have shaped the present day, most notably Margaret Thatcher and Ronald Reagan.

ABOUT THE AUTHOR OF THE ORIGINAL WORK

Born in Vienna, Austria, in 1899, **Friedrich Hayek** would go on to found the influential Austrian Institute of Economic Research. After teaching at the London School of Economics in the 1930s, Hayek became a British subject in 1938, the year Austria was annexed by Adolf Hitler's Germany. Hayek was concerned about how tyranny could develop out of excessive government control of economic planning. This led him to write *The Road to Serfdom*. Hayek would become one of the most influential political economists of the twentieth century. He died in 1992 at the age of 92.

ABOUT THE AUTHOR OF THE ANALYSIS

David Linden is doing postgraduate work on the new right at King's College London. He works as an editor at Svenskt Militärhistoriskt Bibliotek in Stockholm.

Nick Broten was educated at the California Institute of Technology and the London School of Economics. He is doing postgraduate work at the Pardee RAND Graduate School and works as an assistant policy analyst at RAND. His current policy interests include designing distribution methods for end-of-life care, closing labour market skill gaps, and understanding biases in risk-taking by venture capitalists.

ABOUT MACAT

GREAT WORKS FOR CRITICAL THINKING

Macat is focused on making the ideas of the world's great thinkers accessible and comprehensible to everybody, everywhere, in ways that promote the development of enhanced critical thinking skills.

It works with leading academics from the world's top universities to produce new analyses that focus on the ideas and the impact of the most influential works ever written across a wide variety of academic disciplines. Each of the works that sit at the heart of its growing library is an enduring example of great thinking. But by setting them in context – and looking at the influences that shaped their authors, as well as the responses they provoked – Macat encourages readers to look at these classics and game-changers with fresh eyes. Readers learn to think, engage and challenge their ideas, rather than simply accepting them.

'Macat offers an amazing first-of-its-kind tool for interdisciplinary learning and research. Its focus on works that transformed their disciplines and its rigorous approach, drawing on the world's leading experts and educational institutions, opens up a world-class education to anyone.'

Andreas Schleicher,
Director for Education and Skills, Organisation for Economic
Co-operation and Development

'Macat is taking on some of the major challenges in university education ... They have drawn together a strong team of active academics who are producing teaching materials that are novel in the breadth of their approach.'

Prof Lord Broers,
former Vice-Chancellor of the University of Cambridge

'The Macat vision is exceptionally exciting. It focuses upon new modes of learning which analyse and explain seminal texts which have profoundly influenced world thinking and so social and economic development. It promotes the kind of critical thinking which is essential for any society and economy.
This is the learning of the future.'

Rt Hon Charles Clarke, former UK Secretary of State for Education

'The Macat analyses provide immediate access to the critical conversation surrounding the books that have shaped their respective discipline, which will make them an invaluable resource to all of those, students and teachers, working in the field.'

Professor William Tronzo, University of California at San Diego

WAYS IN TO THE TEXT

KEY POINTS

- Friedrich Hayek (1899–1992) was an Austrian British economist whose work covered the history of socialism,* the uses of knowledge in society, and the role of prices in the economy.

- Published in 1944, *The Road to Serfdom* is a challenge to socialism and planned economies* more generally, arguing that such planning inevitably leads to the erosion of democracy* and individual freedom.

- *The Road to Serfdom* asks a fundamental question linking economics and government: How should the economy be run to maintain democracy and the overall well-being of the people?

Who was Friedrich Hayek?

Friedrich Hayek was an Austrian-born, naturalized British* economist considered to be one of the most important social theorists of the twentieth century. He was well known for supporting classic liberalism*—the political philosophy based on the protection of individual liberties and limited government—and the belief that free-market economies* and democratic societies operate in tandem.

Born in Vienna in 1899, Hayek earned a doctorate in law at the University of Vienna in 1921 and another in political science in 1923.

In 1927, with the help of fellow economist Ludwig von Mises,* Hayek founded the Austrian Institute of Economic Research,* which was dedicated to studying fluctuations in markets. Markets refer to the many environments in which people can exchange goods and services, from farmers' markets to the New York Stock Exchange. Markets fluctuate when the demand for goods exceeds the supply, or vice versa.

In 1931 Hayek moved to London, where he joined the faculty of the London School of Economics.* He remained at the LSE until 1950. This move from continental Europe to Britain is significant, as the ideas Hayek put forward in *The Road to Serfdom* were in some ways a warning to Britain about what he had seen happening in neighboring Germany while he was in Vienna, during the Nazi* party's rise to power.

After Britain, Hayek then moved to the United States to take up a post in the department of economics at the University of Chicago. He eventually moved back to Europe in 1962 to work in Germany at the University of Freiburg, where he finished his academic career.

Outside of his academic work, Hayek was always active in politics, influencing British Prime Minister Margaret Thatcher* and United States President Ronald Reagan,* both personally and through his writings. Their policies aimed at cutting government spending were strongly tied to Hayek's ideas as put forward in *The Road to Serfdom*.[1]

What Does The Road to Serfdom *Say*?

The Road to Serfdom addresses one of the most important problems in economics: How should the economy be run to maintain democracy and the overall well-being of the people? Students of all academic disciplines will at some point have to develop an opinion, however broad, on this question. You can't vote in a knowledgeable way for any party without making your mind up on what you think is an acceptable level of government interference in the economy. The book is an excellent introduction to a point of view that sees government control of the economy as dangerous to individual freedom. This is a viewpoint that has grown in popularity in the aftermath of the financial crisis of 2007–8,* as some of the governmental responses to the crisis—most notably, the passing of the bill known as the Federal Stimulus Package*—awakened fears of governments   interfering too much.

The book also helps readers to better understand a crucial period in political and intellectual history. Many of the economic institutions that are still important today, such as the World Bank* and the International Monetary Fund,* were established around the time *The Road to Serfdom* was published. These institutions, as well as many government programs such as national health insurance* and the welfare state,* have their roots in the cataclysmic events that preceded them, particularly the Great Depression* and World War II.

To have a detailed understanding of today's global economy, it is important to have some idea about the debates that shaped the period when Hayek was writing *The Road to Serfdom*. Of these debates, one of the most important concerned the appropriate size and influence of the state. Hayek's contribution to the debate will challenge people to think deeply about these issues, whatever their political beliefs may be. Those drawn towards the idea of free markets and smaller governments will find in Hayek's book intellectual ammunition to strengthen their views and place them in a wider historical context. Those with sympathy for aspects of the welfare state will be forced to examine their thinking when faced with such a powerful challenge.

The force of Hayek's arguments is highlighted by the fact that even his natural political opponents found them compelling. The economist John Maynard Keynes,* whose fundamental ideas included the necessity for the government to manage the economy in times of high unemployment, wrote the following about *The Road to Serfdom* (and it appears on the book's cover):"It is a grand book ... Morally and philosophically I find myself in agreement with virtually the whole of it; and not only in agreement, but in deeply moved agreement." Not everybody will reach the same conclusion as Keynes, but everybody will benefit from the experience of reading *The Road to Serfdom*.

Why Does The Road to Serfdom Matter?

We Now Know argues that the new documentary evidence that had come from the former Soviet Union and its allies since the end of the Cold War changed how the conflict should be understood historically. The title of the book is important, as the main aim of *We Now Know* was to explain what "we"—that is, Gaddis and his readers—"now know" about the Cold War. The title was an invitation to readers to join Gaddis on a journey through the new history of the Cold War. The author's interpretation of the new documents and evidence would make it clear what he believed people now knew about the Cold War (as opposed what people thought they knew before this evidence was available), why it started, how it escalated and why it went on for so long.

When *We Now Know* was published, it was an exciting time for Cold War research. The consensus view was that the collapse of the Soviet Union meant an end to the Cold War, allowing the first histories of the entire period of conflict to be written. Given the slew of new documents from the former Soviet Union and its allies in Eastern Europe and China, researchers had the opportunity to write histories from a fully international perspective. This, of course, had a significant effect on both Gaddis's decision to write *We Now Know* and on the conclusions that he came to—as he admits in the book's preface, acknowledging the debt he owed to the work of other historians in the course of researching and writing his study.

We Now Know is a landmark work on the struggle for political and ideological supremacy between the United States and the Soviet Union during the second half of the twentieth century. Looking at the conflict from its early beginnings through to the Cuban Missile Crisis* of October 1962 (the closest the Cold War came to a "hot" war fought with nuclear weapons), its use of newly available documents from both Western and communist nations and its novel interpretation of events establish it as a key work of so–called "new Cold War history."

NOTES

1   Glenn Beck, "Is US Traveling Down 'Road to Serfdom?'" *Fox News*, http://www.foxnews.com/story/2010/06/09/glenn-beck-is-us-traveling-down-road-to-serfdom/, accessed March 6, 2015.

SECTION 1
INFLUENCES

MODULE 1
THE AUTHOR AND THE HISTORICAL CONTEXT

KEY POINTS

- *The Road to Serfdom* is a key work in the study of political and economic institutions, particularly in the debate between market-based and planned economies.*

- Friedrich Hayek witnessed first-hand the emergence of totalitarianism* in Europe, and wanted to write a book warning Britain of the dangers of totalitarian rule.

- Hayek was an economist, but he was concerned about the wider effects of too much government intervention in economic planning.

Why Read this Text?

Friedrich Hayek lived between 1899 and 1992, and his 1944 book *The Road to Serfdom* is one of the most popular economics works of the twentieth century. It remains an important part of economic and political debate today. Its central argument—that planned economies inevitably lead to reductions in individual freedom and eventually to totalitarian rule—has played a significant role in the politics of the United States and Europe since its publication, inspiring leaders such as Ronald Reagan* and Margaret Thatcher* to put in place policies intended to shrink the state and limit the role of government in economic life. Politicians and commentators still frequently refer to the book as a warning against excessive government power.

The most pessimistic part of Hayek's argument is not, however, supported by any evidence. As the economist Robert Solow* writes: "It would be perverse to read the history, as of 1944 or as of now, as

> **❝** It is true that the virtues which are less esteemed
> and practiced now—independence, self-reliance, and
> the willingness to bear risks, the readiness to back one's
> own conviction against a majority, and the willingness
> to voluntary cooperation with one's neighbors—
> are essentially those on which the working of an
> individualist society rests. Collectivism has nothing
> to put in their place, and in so far as it already has
> destroyed them it has left a void filled by nothing but
> the demand for obedience and the compulsion of the
> individual to what is collectively decided to be good. **❞**
>
> Friedrich Hayek, *The Road to Serfdom*

suggesting that the standard regulatory interventions in the economy have any inherent tendency to snowball into 'serfdom' … Hayek's implicit prediction is a failure."[1] In this way, Hayek's suggestion that the rule of law* and democracy* are incompatible with government interference in the economy may well have been proven to be false. Even so, it is still true that the book has played a real role in shifting the balance of economic power from the state to the markets, particularly in Britain and the United States.

Author's Life
Hayek was born in Vienna and was educated as an economist in both Austria and the United States. In 1931 he moved to Britain, where he was appointed professor of economics at the London School of Economics and Political Science (LSE).* He worked there until 1950, when he moved to the United States to become professor of economics at the University of Chicago, then in 1962 he moved to Freiburg University in Germany, where he spent the rest of his academic career. Jointly with the Swedish economist Gunnar Myrdal,

Hayek received the Nobel Memorial Prize in Economic Sciences[2] in 1974. Both Hayek and Myrdal studied the relationship between economics and the social and political sciences,* which is where the study of society and government meet. Apparently, the Prize Committee "initially intended to award the prize to Myrdal but was persuaded to balance his support for significant government involvement in the economy by choosing Hayek to share the prize."[3]

The Road to Serfdom was written during World War II,* when the lse had been evacuated out of London to Peterhouse College at Cambridge University. During the war Hayek was not a part of the British war effort, despite having become a naturalized British* citizen in 1938. For that reason, he had more time to write, as teaching was partially suspended because of the war. At this time he also felt he "had come to master English, in the sense that [he] got enjoyment in writing in English."[4] Hayek's experience of reading and working in both German and English allowed him to bring some of the Austrian ideas associated with economics to an English-speaking audience in London.

Author's Background

The Road to Serfdom was shaped by political events in Europe between World War I* and World War II. This period was one of great intellectual and social upheaval, leading to the rise of both socialist* and fascist* political movements throughout Europe. Hayek witnessed first-hand the development of anti-democratic forces in Vienna after World War I, at a time when attempts to create a democratic state in Austria had resulted in both Communists and National Socialists (Nazis)* gaining political influence. For example, the University of Vienna, where Hayek studied in the 1920s, was fertile ground for anti-democratic ideas and was temporarily shut down due to conflict. He feared that after World War II Britain would succumb to similar anti-democratic forces as a result of increased government powers. In *The*

Road to Serfdom, he warned that "there is more than a superficial similarity between the trend of thought in Germany during and after the last war [i.e. World War I] and the present current of ideas in the democracies."[5]

The book was written as a guidebook for the British economy after World War II. When the text was written, in 1944, the thrust of intellectual thought in Britain was towards economic planning, where the government plays a much more active role in directing the economy. The entire Labour Party* and certain elements within the Conservative Party* in Great Britain agreed that there should be a greater interest in economic planning. These were not fixed ideas, but it was generally accepted that things could not go the same way as they had after World War I, when economic depression and unemployment had quickly set in. For that reason, the wartime coalition* government commissioned the economist and social reformer William Beveridge* to write a report on how the post-war state should be organized. The Beveridge Report* is commonly thought to have signaled the beginning of the British welfare state.* *The Road to Serfdom* is, therefore, the result of Hayek feeling alienated from what he saw as creeping socialism in Britain, as well as of his concerns about the implications of totalitarianism.

NOTES

1   Robert Solow, "Hayek, Friedman, and the Illusions of Conservative Economics," *New Republic*, http://www.newrepublic.com/article/books-and-arts/magazine/110196/hayek-friedman-and-the-illusions-conservative-economics last accessed March 5, 2015.

2   Gunnar Wetterberg, *Pengarna & Makten: Riksbankens historia* (Stockholm: Sveriges Riksbank i samarbete med Atlantis, 2009), 374.

3   Marilu Hurt-McCarty, *The Nobel Laureates: How the World's Greatest Economic Minds Shaped Modern Thought* (New York: McGraw-Hill, 2000), 242.

4   F. A. Hayek, *Hayek on Hayek: An Autobiographical Dialogue – The Collected Works of F. A. Hayek*, ed. Stephen Kresge and Leif Wenar (London: Routledge, 1994), 101.

5   F.A. Hayek, *The Road to Serfdom: Texts and Documents – The Definitive Edition*, ed. Bruce Caldwell (Chicago, IL: Chicago University Press, 2008), 58.

MODULE 2
ACADEMIC CONTEXT

KEY POINTS

- Economists try to study the production and distribution of goods in society, often advising governments on how much or how little they should interfere with free markets.*

- Important economists, including Adam Smith, Karl Marx and John Maynard Keynes, all have different ideas on how best an economy can function.

- Hayek was influenced by economist Ludwig von Mises's 1922 work *Socialism: An Economic Analysis.*

The Work In Its Context

Friedrich Hayek's *The Road to Serfdom* is not a normal economics book, because it draws more on history and philosophy than most major works in the field do. Still, the question it poses—how should the economy be run to maintain democracy and overall well-being?—is at the heart of economic thought. Though much of Hayek's reasoning is more political than economic, we should still think of *The Road to Serfdom* as a work of economics.

Economics looks at the production and distribution of goods in society. The economist Lionel Robbins, who helped recruit Hayek to the London School of Economics* in 1931, famously defined economics as "a science which studies human behavior as a relationship between ends and scarce means which have alternative uses."[1] Robbins's definition is both abstract and narrow and it mostly limits the field of study to the exchange of goods and services in society—though it does leave room for interpretation as to what those goods and services might be. Even by the terms of this quite limited

> 66 The curious task of economics is to demonstrate to men how little they really know about what they imagine they can design. 99
> Friedrich Hayek, *The Fatal Conceit*

definition, the study of economics includes a wide range of economic institutions and behaviors: from buying and selling in the market, to the structure of government, to interactions between individuals. Economists study both the small-scale decisions consumers and firms make on a daily basis and the large-scale trends of the economy as a whole.

While—as Robbins suggests in his definition—economists try to study society as scientifically as possible, many economists also try to make practical contributions to public policy to help with the organization of society. One of the main areas in which economists have influenced policymakers is in advising governments on how they should and can interfere with free markets. *The Road to Serfdom* is a particularly strong voice in this debate.

Overview of the Field

The father of modern economics is Adam Smith, whose 1776 book *The Wealth of Nations* was one of the first comprehensive looks at the market system.[2] Smith wrote his book as a reaction to the mercantilist* policies of the time. Under mercantilism, it was widely believed that the most effective way for a country to increase its economic power was to grab as many resources—such as gold—as possible, to protect its trade from competitors. Smith's argument, on the other hand, sowed the seeds of the idea that trade can benefit both parties, whether they are nations or individuals. Smith introduced the idea that individuals who are acting in their own self-interest, can also benefit society through the market, as if they were guided by an "invisible hand."[3]

Perhaps the strongest attack on Smith's argument that markets can naturally be beneficial for society came from the father of communism,* Karl Marx. Marx argued that within the free-market system there were forces that would eventually destabilize and undermine the capitalist* system. Specifically, Marx believed that as wealth in the form of capital became more concentrated in a few hands and wages stagnated, the working class would revolt against this injustice and eventually overturn the capitalistic rich. Marx and his fellow thinker Friedrich Engels developed the idea of communism, the theory of a society built on the idea that the means of production— everything from natural resources to factories—should be owned equally by everyone, not by private individuals or companies. Marx and Engels wrote in the *Communist Manifesto* that "the history of all hitherto existing society is the history of class struggles," and argued that under communism class struggle would be abolished by establishing the final and total victory of the proletariat—the working class.[4]

While Marx developed his version of political economy as a radical attack on free-market capitalism, John Maynard Keynes's version of economics balanced the need for markets with a significant role for the state. Keynes believed that the kind of pro-market story Smith told in *The Wealth of Nations* could work in specialized circumstances, but that markets would frequently fail for a variety of political, structural, and emotional reasons—what he called the "animal spirits" of the economy.[5] To bring the economy back to its productive best in such situations as the Great Depression,* where a society's total level of demand—or aggregate demand*—is low, Keynes was in favor of fiscal stimulus. In other words, he believed governments should spend to stimulate growth. This conversation about what constitutes the right economic blend of markets and the state goes on today, with supporters of Smith, Marx, and Keynes all still active in the debate.

Academic Influences

Major economists like Adam Smith, Karl Marx and John Maynard Keynes all had an influence on Hayek, but other people also inspired him. After World War I* Hayek was studying at the University of Vienna when he came across the Austrian School of Economics, set up by Carl Menger.* Menger had an individualistic approach in economics, believing that the focus of all economic research should lie "in the action, decisions, values, and knowledge of individuals."[6] This view, associated with the Austrian School, is different from both the Smithian and the Marxian traditions, but is a specific challenge to Keynes, who tended to analyze the economy not in terms of individuals, but in terms of society as a whole.

Hayek's contemporary and fellow economist Ludwig von Mises* published a critique of socialism* in 1922 entitled *Socialism: An Economic Analysis*. This book criticized governments that wanted to manage prices because, von Mises thought, without prices naturally adjusting themselves according to conditions, the market would not be able to allocate resources efficiently. One idea in von Mises's book that has a clear connection with Hayek's work concerns the difficulty in maintaining an economy that has some aspects of the free market and some aspects of socialism. As Hayek himself writes concerning the inability of governments to set only some prices and let others adjust freely: "There is no ... social system feasible which would be neither market economy nor socialism."[7]

Nineteenth-century French philosopher Alexis de Tocqueville* was also an influence on Hayek, who chose the title of his book as a subtle reference to the Frenchman. De Tocqueville had himself warned that when the government abandoned the freedom of its citizens as a primary aim, then it was starting on a road that would lead to slavery for its citizens. For Hayek, this was "the road to serfdom."[8]

NOTES

1   Lionel Robbins, *An Essay on the Nature and Significance of Economic Science*, Ludwig von Mises Institute (2007): 15.

2   Adam Smith, *An Inquiry into the Nature and Causes of the Wealth of Nations* (London, 1799).

3   Smith, *Wealth of Nations*, 181.

4   Karl Marx and Friedrich Engels, *The Communist Manifesto* (New York: Simon and Schuster, 1964): 55.

5   John Maynard Keynes, *The General Theory of Employment, Interest, and Money* (London: Macmillan, 1936): 161–2.

6   Alan Ebenstein, *Friedrich Hayek: A Biography* (New York: Palgrave Macmillan, 2001), 24.

7   Ludwig von Mises, *Socialism: An Economic and Sociological Analysis* (Alabama: Ludwig von Mises Institute, 2009): 534.

8   Ebenstein, *Friedrich Hayek*, 116.

MODULE 3
THE PROBLEM

KEY POINTS

- The key question concerning economists and political scientists* at the time Hayek wrote *The Road to Serfdom* was: "What is the proper balance between economic freedom and social justice?"

- Hayek was trying to work out the best way for the economy to help with social needs—and he was not coming from a fixed political viewpoint of right or left.

- Hayek saw threats to freedom when too much control was exerted by the state, whichever political doctrine that state followed.

Core Question

The core question that Friedrich Hayek tries to answer in *The Road to Serfdom* is why political planning*—governments actively participating in shaping a country's economy—is a danger to the concept of democracy.* In other words, how political planning can lead a society to serfdom. This question can be divided into three sub-questions:

- Why was there general sympathy for the concept of political planning at the time?
- How would planning lead to the gradual erosion of democracy and the rule of law?*
- How would this erosion of democracy eventually lead to a dictatorship that was indistinguishable from fascism*—an important concern at the time as the British public observed the consequences of fascism in Germany.

> **❝** It is almost universally felt that when we call a country democratic we are praising it; consequently, the defenders of every kind of regime claim that it is a democracy, and fear that they might have to stop using the word if it were tied down to any one meaning. **❞**
>
> George Orwell, *Politics and the English Language*

Hayek answers the first question with an account of how classical liberalism* at the beginning of the twentieth century was seen to have failed, leading to it becoming unfashionable in the world of politics. It had been replaced by socialism, which appealed to people because it offered a vision of a utopian society which classical liberalism suggested was not possible.

Responding to the second question, Hayek shows how planning leads to an erosion of democracy by gradually increasing the authority of the government at the expense of democratic institutions.

Finally, Hayek approaches the third question, about fears of dictatorship, by examining how democracy was already held in contempt in much British public debate of the time.

The core question—why political planning threatens democracy—is important because, by the time *The Road to Serfdom* was written, Europe had witnessed the transformation of democratic societies into dictatorships—fascist in Germany, communist in Russia. Hayek also wanted to address the fact that there were still people in the democracies that were left at the time who held views that were similar to those that had brought about dictatorships. He wasn't the only person thinking this either, since "by 1940 no thoughtful person anywhere in the world could keep from wondering what had gone wrong." Hayek, however, was driven to investigate *why* things had gone so badly wrong.[1]

The Participants

At the time *The Road to Serfdom* was published in 1944, the argument among intellectuals was between those who were in favor of an enlarged state—or more state involvement in the economy—and those who wanted to maintain the pre-war size of the state. This was not just a division between the political left and right wings; the depression* of the 1930s had convinced Conservative* politicians such as future Prime Minister Harold Macmillan* that a middle way between left and right was needed. In 1938 Macmillan even published *The Middle Way*, in which he proposed a minimum wage and insurance for the unemployed. *The Road To Serfdom* was shaped by this sense of the necessity for agreement between left and right. Hayek was addressing the book "to the socialists of all parties." Like fellow Austrian economist Ludwig von Mises,* Hayek wasn't sure it was possible to construct a society comprised of some elements of central planning and some of free markets.

In addition to von Mises, Hayek was also influenced by the philosopher Karl Popper,* whose 1945 book *The Open Society and Its Enemies* developed similar themes to *The Road to Serfdom*. According to Canadian philosopher Calvin Hayes, who has compared and contrasted the ideas of both men, Popper was interested in "what he later called 'objective knowledge'" and Hayek was "concerned with subjective knowledge and how it affects economic authors."[2] Popper believed knowledge was objective in the sense that it represented some kind of truth. Hayek, on the other hand, believed human perceptions of the objective world were by their nature incomplete. Both were concerned with how society wanted to limit the level of freedom within it. In the words of British philosopher Norman P. Berry, "the Great Society—that is Hayek's name for Popper's Open Society—is characterized by a very high level of abstraction of its rules. An abstract rule could be 'political freedom' or 'human rights.' In comparison, the rules of a primitive society are specific and concrete—you must not steal, for instance."[3] You could argue, then, that *The Road to Serfdom* and *The Open Society and Its Enemies* are very similar to each other and came from the same intellectual environment. When Popper received a copy of *The Road to Serfdom* he wrote to Hayek: "You were driven by fundamentally the same experience which made me write my book."[4]

The Contemporary Debate

People who were disillusioned with the idea of socialism* had focused on the Soviet Union, although it was mostly journalists who were looking into the subject. People would not start writing about abandoning socialism, however, until during and after World War II,* notably with the 1941 publication of *Darkness at Noon* by the Hungarian émigré and playwright Arthur Koestler* and with George Orwell's* novels *Animal Farm* (1945) and *Nineteen Eighty-Four* (1949). Hayek's contribution to the debate follows on from these writings. As a European refugee he wanted to warn a British audience about developments in continental Europe. *The Road to Serfdom* is part of this tradition, then, but it is also unique in its academic ambition. While Orwell used the power of narrative storytelling to imagine a world where freedom was suppressed, Hayek simply used arguments to make the same points.

According to Hayek's biographer Alan Ebenstein, *The Road to Serfdom* was an attempt "to reach beyond his fellow economists to a wider audience of social scientists and intellectuals."[5] It was also an attempt to reach a wider non-intellectual audience of men and women who had taken part in the war effort and to convince them that the idea of planning was wrong. Originally, Hayek had wanted to compare Nazi* Germany with the Soviet Union* to show the similarities between Nazism and socialism, but was stopped from doing so when the Soviet Union joined the Allies* in the war against Germany in 1941 because such comparisons between the enemy and an ally could jeopardize Britain's war effort. Therefore, Hayek focused on Nazi Germany, even though he thought the Soviet Union was worse "in its suppression of dissenting opinions."[6]

NOTES

1   Stephen Kresge, Introduction to F.A. Hayek, *Hayek on Hayek: An Autobiographical Dialogue – The Collected Works of F.A. Hayek*, ed. Stephen Kresge and Leif Wenar (London: Routledge, 1994), 15.

2   Calvin Hayes, *Popper, Hayek and the Open Society* (London: Routledge, 2009), 67.

3   Norman P. Barry, *Hayek's Social and Economic Philosophy* (London: Macmillan, 1979), 81.

4   Alan Ebenstein, *Friedrich Hayek: A Biography* (New York: PalgraveMacmillan, 2001), 160.

5   Ebenstein, *Friedrich Hayek*, 115.

6   Ebenstein, *Friedrich Hayek*, 141.

THE AUTHOR'S CONTRIBUTION

KEY POINTS

- Hayek argues that democracy* can only function when supported by a free-market economy.*

- It could be argued that The Road to Serfdom was more a book about a political debate at the time than an academic work about the economy.

- Many economists were looking at the issue of whether a planned economy* was a good thing, but only Hayek's book appealed to a wide audience.

Author's Aims

Friedrich Hayek's main aim in writing *The Road to Serfdom* was to attack "what [he] called classical socialism,* aimed mainly at the nationalization or socialization of the means of production."[1] Hayek believed democracy could only survive when it was "allied with freedom of choice that inheres [i.e. exists] in a market system."[2]

Hayek had intended the work to be part of a book project he had begun planning in the 1930s that he referred to as *The Abuse of Reason*. *The Road to Serfdom* was supposed to be the second in a three-part series, the first titled *Hubris of Reason* and the third *The Nemesis of the Planned Society*, neither of which were ever completed.

Although Hayek did not follow the original aims of the project, he did succeed in making the book both a critique of and a warning against future planning,* which he believed led to totalitarianism*. *The Road to Serfdom* is part of a logical plan to attack socialism and warn against government control, using the concrete examples of

> **❝** When Hitler came into power in Germany, I had already been teaching at the University of London for several years, but I kept in close touch with affairs on the Continent and was able to do so until the outbreak of war. What I had thus seen of the origins and evolution of various totalitarian movements made me feel that English public opinion, particularly among my friends who held 'advanced' views on social matters, completely misconceived the nature of those movements. **❞**
>
> Friedrich Hayek, *The Road to Serfdom*

Germany and the Soviet Union.* It departs from the original aims of the *Abuse of Reason* project because it doesn't provide an alternative to classical socialism, so it could be argued that it is more of a polemic, or an attack, rather than a manifesto—a plan for what should happen.

Approach

In addressing his core questions, Hayek's focus is on Germany and on similar ideologies that were present in Britain at the time, though there are also several references to the Soviet Union. In each chapter of *The Road to Serfdom* the core question—concerning why political planning threatens democracy—is addressed with references and opening quotations. The major weakness of this approach is that the book's style gradually falls into the category of contemporary political debate rather than into that of academic enquiry. Hayek is intent on discussing the general character of the topic, and to this extent this book is different from previous works.

In one sense, making a connection between German fascism* and socialism in Britain was the secret of the book's success. At the time it was published, during World War II* in 1944, British citizens were all too aware of the dangers of fascism. The dangers of socialism, on the other hand, were much farther from public consciousness.

Hayek did not shy away from being argumentative, and the book's tone often reflects how serious things were at the time. According to the British newspaper *The Times*, Hayek's "most famous book now seems unduly gloomy about the prospects of a collapse of civil society under the burden of the welfare state."[3] But the author succeeded in producing a work that was a warning, not a prediction. Hayek also accepted that the book was certain to "offend many people with whom [he wished] to live on friendly terms."[4] In 1956, he said that at first "the book was taken in the spirit in which it was written,"[5] though he was fully prepared for the academic criticism the book received in Britain.

Contribution In Context

The Road to Serfdom does not contain a set of ideas that are Hayek's alone. According to British historian Richard Cockett, with the renewed interest in "the planning *versus* private enterprise debate, many economists rushed into print on the subject towards the end of the war."[6] Economists who were against planning all agreed that it would be a danger to democracy but Hayek's is the only work that became popular with the wider public, influencing public opinion on a large scale. It is unique because it is aimed at a wider audience than just economists, and presents the reader with an understanding of European, British and American philosophy, history and economic thought.

In some ways, the book was ahead of its time. In 1944, the most widely held view was that capitalism* was in crisis and that central planning was a workable alternative to ease the suffering caused by the capitalist system. The book set out to speak to a huge number of young men and women who had learned to distrust capitalism in the 1930s because of the economic depression and the unemployment it had brought. Hayek succeeded in reaching his target audience and, in 1944, an initial print run of 2,000 copies of *The Road to Serfdom* sold out within a month. The text was also quoted in parliament, which led to

Hayek being invited to lecture in the United States. The University of Chicago Press estimated in the introduction to the 2007 edition that 350,000 copies of the book had been sold to date.[7]

NOTES

1   F. A. Hayek, *Hayek on Hayek: An Autobiographical Dialogue – The Collected Works of F. A. Hayek*, ed. Stephen Kresge and Leif Wenar (London: Routledge, 1994), 108.

2   Bruce Caldwell, *Hayek's Challenge: An Intellectual Biography of F. A. Hayek* (Chicago, IL: University of Chicago Press, 2004), 240.

3   "Maestro of Economics," *The Times*, March 25, 1992.

4   F. A. Hayek, "Preface to the Original Editions," in F. A. Hayek, *The Road to Serfdom: Texts and Documents – The Definitive Edition*, ed. Bruce Caldwell (Chicago, IL: Chicago University Press, 2008), 37

5   F.A. Hayek, "Foreword to the 1956 American Paperback Edition," in Hayek, *The Road to Serfdom*, 238.

6   Richard Cockett, *Thinking the Unthinkable: Think Tanks and the Economic Counter-Revolution, 1931–1983* (London: HarperCollins, 1994), 79.

7   "The Publication History of *The Road to Serfdom*," University of Chicago Press website, excerpted from Bruce Caldwell, "Introduction," in Hayek, *The Road to Serfdom*, http://press.uchicago.edu/Misc/Chicago/320553.html, accessed January 25, 2014.

SECTION 2
IDEAS

MAIN IDEAS

KEY POINTS

- The key themes of *The Road to Serfdom* are the "attractions" of socialism,* the danger of economic planning,* and the historical evolution of socialism, particularly in Britain.

- Hayek's core argument is that planned economies, despite their good intentions, eventually lead to the erosion of freedom and democracy.*

- The book is generally seen as an attack on socialism rather than as an endorsement of classical liberalism.*

Key Themes

The main themes of *The Road to Serfdom* are made clear by Friedrich Hayek's organization of the book into three distinct parts. First he discusses what people think of as the attraction of socialism. In promising a utopia,* socialism had replaced liberalism* "as the doctrine held by the great majority of progressives."[1] Hayek argues that in fact socialism leads to the erosion of freedom, meaning that "to strive for it produces something so utterly different that few of those who now wish it would be prepared to accept the consequences."[2] Second, Hayek addresses the danger of planning.* With planning, "the state ceases to be a piece of utilitarian machinery … and becomes a 'moral' institution … which imposes on its members its views on all moral questions, whether these views be moral or highly immoral."[3] When the government controls the moral direction in society—effectively deciding what is right and what is wrong—it moves towards totalitarianism.*[4] Finally, Hayek turns to signs of socialism in British

> 66 If in the first attempt to create a world of free men
> we have failed, we must try again. The guiding principle
> that a policy of freedom for the individual is the only
> truly progressive policy remains as true today as it was
> in the nineteenth century. 99
>
> Friedrich Hayek, *The Road to Serfdom*

society. He sees "the increasing veneration for the state" as a sign of increased totalitarianism. He also shows how people who fought Hitler had a positive view of socialism as well, despite the fact that, as far as Hayek is concerned, socialism and Nazism* share the same totalitarian foundation.

The book is organized chronologically, its 16 chapters covering the following three themes:

- The apparent attraction of socialism to a post-war society.
- The danger to a democratic society of economic planning.
- Creeping totalitarianism in British society—the book providing an assessment of the different signs of this phenomenon.

Within this framework, each of the 16 chapters can be read separately without the need to read the whole book.

Exploring The Ideas

Hayek's core argument is that classical socialism inevitably leads to the erosion of freedom and democracy. From the start, he draws a comparison between the German Nazi regime and what he sees as the real threat of totalitarianism in Britain, writing: "The very magnitude of the outrages committed by the National Socialists has strengthened the assurance that a totalitarian system cannot happen here."[5] However, Hayek then goes on to say that "in the democracies at present, many who sincerely hate all of Nazism's manifestations are working for ideals whose realization would lead straight to the abhorred tyranny."[6]

At the center of Hayek's argument is the fact that there are ways in which power can be corrupted in a classical socialist system, as in the use of central planning to control the economy. For him, planners "have the tragic illusion" that by transferring economic power from individuals to society they "extinguish that power" and the chance that it can be corrupted. Hayek believes it is "not only transformed, but infinitely heightened."[7] This view—that planned economies concentrate the power of society into far fewer hands than a system driven by private enterprise—is captured in a single statement: "To decentralize power is to reduce the absolute amount of power, and the competitive system is the only system designed to minimize the power exercised by man over man."[8] In other words, to take economic power away from a central authority and let the market decide is the only way to reduce the power of one person over another.

Because planning tends to concentrate power by telling consumers and producers what they can buy and sell, Hayek argues that planned economies eventually lead to dictatorships. He says this because dictatorship* is the "most effective instrument of coercion and, as such, essential if central planning on a large scale is to be possible."[9]

The idea that freedom and socialism are incompatible underpins Hayek's suggestion that planning always leads to dictatorship. He argues that socialism actually changed the meaning of freedom in order to "harness to its cart the strongest of all political motives—the craving for freedom."[10] Instead of seeing individual freedom as "freedom from coercion" or the ability to act as you like in both political and economic life, Hayek says that socialists redefined freedom as "freedom from necessity."[11] The "false hope" that a planned economy would produce more economic output than the capitalist system is as powerful "as anything which drives us along the road to planning."[12] Throughout this whole argument, Hayek's clear target is the British leadership and the British public.

Language And Expression

Hayek was aware that *The Road to Serfdom* was a polemical—that is, a controversial and critical—work. The book is mostly seen as an attack on socialism, rather than as an endorsement of classical liberalism. Its failure to show both aspects of Hayek's message clearly is something of an obstacle to understanding the work, though not an i nsurmountable one.

Still, *The Road to Serfdom* should be seen as part of the debate between classical socialism and classical liberalism. Hayek identified himself clearly with the latter. The main criticism of the book is that Hayek makes too much of the danger of government planning. His overriding focus on this also leads him to ignore the issue of high taxation and its impact on certain aspects of socialist thinking. In the preface to the 1976 edition of the book, Hayek tries to put this mistake right by saying that there are two kinds of socialism: classical socialism, which focuses on government planning; and redistributive socialism, which looks to high taxes and a large welfare state.* Hayek believed that both schools led to the same negative outcome. But his ignorance of social democratic* societies, such as Sweden and West Germany, where his predicted negative outcomes didn't materialize, could be seen as one of the book's most serious flaws.

NOTES

1   F. A. Hayek, *The Road to Serfdom: Texts and Documents – The Definitive Edition*, ed. Bruce Caldwell (Chicago, IL: Chicago University Press, 2008), 76.

2   Hayek, *The Road to Serfdom*, 82.

3   Hayek, *The Road to Serfdom*, 115.

4   Hayek, *The Road to Serfdom*, 194.

5   F. A. Hayek, *The Road to Serfdom—Condensed Version* (Reader's Digest, 1999), 39.

6   Hayek, *The Road to Serfdom—Condensed Version*, 40.

7   Hayek, *The Road to Serfdom—Condensed Version*, 40.

8   Hayek, *The Road to Serfdom—Condensed Version*, 41.

9   Hayek, *The Road to Serfdom—Condensed Version*, 50.

10 Hayek, *The Road to Serfdom—Condensed Version*, 47.

11 Hayek, *The Road to Serfdom—Condensed Version*, 48.

12 Hayek, *The Road to Serfdom—Condensed Version*, 48.

SECONDARY IDEAS

KEY POINTS

- Hayek argued that planned economies* produce poor political leaders—that planning is incompatible with the rule of law.*

- He believes that socialist* rule itself depends on undemocratic methods.

- Hayek says people are allowed to fail in a free society, whereas in a society with excessive government control, failure would need to be punished.

Other Ideas

Hayek's book holds together as a coherent and persuasive work, with all of his secondary ideas that are there adding weight to his main theory. In general, Hayek's ideas do not follow one from another—they stand alone—so it isn't vital to understand his secondary ideas to absorb the central idea. Still, the richness of Hayek's overall critique of socialism is that it is built on all of his smaller attacks.

The Road to Serfdom tackles a secondary idea that planned societies produce the worst kind of political leaders. This is because socialism needs power to be centralized if it is to exercise authority. Hayek believes this creates a system with "a degree of dependency scarcely distinguished from slavery."[1] It is a system where the leaders "must create power—power over men wielded by other men—of a magnitude never before known."[2] Hayek also looks at how incompatible planning* is with the Anglo-Saxon idea of the rule of law. He defines the rule of law as a set of "rules fixed and announced beforehand." Contrary to this, planning would, he believes, create a

> **❝** We were the first to assert that the more complicated the form assumed by civilization, the more restricted the freedom of the individual must become. **❞**
> Benito Mussolini, Grand Fascist Council Report

system of arbitrary—or seemingly random—policies that are constantly changing to fit the needs of the government.[3]

Exploring The Ideas

Hayek's secondary ideas help to back up his main argument that planned societies lead to freedom being eroded. The first two of these secondary ideas—that planned societies produce abusive leaders and are incompatible with the rule of law—come from Hayek's own intellectual background. At the University of Vienna, he witnessed both academic purges and the erosion of the rule of law by political groups, and became a strong defender of the idea of having established rules that could not be challenged. Both of these are expressed in a clear and direct way in order to underline the book's main message.

In his discussion of what it takes to be a leader in planned economies, Hayek also claims that socialist rule requires undemocratic methods: "The old socialist parties were inhibited by their democratic ideals; they did not possess the ruthlessness required for the performance of their chosen task."[4] In order for socialist regimes to work properly, according to Hayek, "the question can no longer be on what do a majority of the people agree but what the largest single group is whose members agree sufficiently to make unified direction of all affairs possible." So the logic of rule in a socialist regime is back to front: rather than reaching a compromise on the issues, leaders must find a leadership group in which compromise is unnecessary.

Hayek says this attracts poor leaders to socialist regimes for three reasons. First, people who are more intelligent will understand the idea and value of many and varied opinions, and so "if we wish to find a high degree of uniformity in outlook, we have to descend to the regions of lower moral and intellectual standards." Second, increasing the size of the group requires converting others to a "simple creed," which will attract the "docile and gullible."[5] Finally, Hayek argues that "it seems to be easier for people to agree on a negative program," and so socialist organizations must build on the exploitation of human weakness rather than on a positive vision.[6]

Hayek's argument that socialism is incompatible with the rule of law relies on a similar logic. To him, the rule of law is defined as "the absence of legal privileges of particular people designated by authority." It protects citizens from "arbitrary government" of the kind defined by the Nazi* regime.[7] When governments have to plan for everything in the economy—for example, how many pigs to raise—they must make decisions that balance the interests of multiple groups in society, and this necessarily interferes with the rule of law.

Overlooked

There is no real reason to reinterpret *The Road to Serfdom* today. The major theme of the text—that excessive government planning endangers freedom in society and therefore the existence of democracy—has stood the test of time and can be applied in a modern context. However, there are three areas of the book (Chapters 1–7 and 9) that have been neglected, where Hayek discusses security and freedom, material conditions and ideal ends, and the prospects of an international order.

On the subject of security and freedom, Hayek expresses support for "some minimum of food, shelter, and clothing, sufficient to preserve health and the capacity to work" for everyone.[8] He rejects demands for greater social security, arguing that this would work as an obstacle to people's freedom of employment. He backs this up with a quotation from the twentieth-century German philosopher William

Roepke: "The last resort of a competitive economy is the bailiff, the ultimate sanction of a planned economy is the hangman."[9] By this he means that in a free society, people are allowed to fail, while in a society that is not free, the government would have to punish failure. In other words, in order for a society to be truly free, the institutions of that society must ensure that a certain amount of the material well-being of its citizens is left up to circumstance and chance, and is not prescribed by excessive social security.

With reference to material conditions and society's ideal ends, Hayek wanted "to defend the ideals which our enemies attack." He believed that supporters of what he called the "traditions which have made England and America countries of free and upright, tolerant and independent, people"—people who believe in individual liberty and free enterprise—must defend themselves against "new totalitarian* ideas."[10] Hayek urges his readers to maintain an "unwavering faith" in this "traditional" way of life and not to compromise.

Hayek also wrote about the international order and its prospects in the years after World War II: "In no other field has the world yet paid so dearly for the abandonment of nineteenth-century liberalism."[11] This is because international relations at this time looked like they would depend more and more on increased government planning. Hayek warned that "we must not believe that we can at one stroke create a permanent organisation which will make all wars in any part of the world entirely impossible."[12] Here it is likely that he was referring to the United Nations, established in 1945 to promote international cooperation.

NOTES

1   F. A. Hayek, *The Road to Serfdom: Texts and Documents – The Definitive Edition*, ed. Bruce Caldwell (Chicago, IL: Chicago University Press, 2008), 166.

2   Hayek, *The Road to Serfdom*, 165.

3   F. A. Hayek, *The Road to Serfdom—Condensed Version* (Reader's Digest, 1999), 57.

4   Hayek, *The Road to Serfdom—Condensed Version*, 52.

5   Hayek, *The Road to Serfdom—Condensed Version*, 53.

6   Hayek, *The Road to Serfdom—Condensed Version*, 53.

7   Hayek, *The Road to Serfdom—Condensed Version*, 58.

8   Hayek, *The Road to Serfdom*, 148.

9   Hayek, *The Road to Serfdom*, 151–2.

10 Hayek, *The Road to Serfdom*, 222.

11 Hayek, *The Road to Serfdom*, 223.

12 Hayek, *The Road to Serfdom*, 236.

MODULE 7
ACHIEVEMENT

KEY POINTS

- Hayek was very successful in presenting a challenge to socialism* that would be heard by the world.

- Conservatives* still refer to *The Road to Serfdom* when they are looking to oppose a government's role in the economy.

- To fully understand the book, readers need to have a relatively deep background knowledge of Hayek and the times he experienced.

Assessing The Argument

Friedrich Hayek was very successful in *The Road to Serfdom* in achieving his core aim of presenting an intellectual challenge to socialism.* The aftershocks of that challenge can still be felt today in policy discussions, as well as in the academic world. The book has had a huge influence in a number of disciplines, including history, economics and philosophy. It does not fit firmly within one single discipline, and scholars in a number of different areas have explored and adopted its ideas. Public choice theory*—the idea that politicians and members of the public sector act out of self-interest,* just like those in the private sector—is an attempt to apply classical liberal economics to political science, and it can be traced back to Hayek's ideas. *The Road to Serfdom* has been called "an excellent example of early Austrian contribution to public choice theory" because Hayek showed that one effect of socialism "is evident in the growth of special interest groups."[1] In other words, focusing on the incentives of planners in a socialist society, Hayek described how governmental

> ❝ Over the years, I have again and again asked fellow believers in a free society how they managed to escape the contagion of their collectivist intellectual environment. No name has been mentioned more often as the source of enlightenment and understanding than Friedrich Hayek's. I, like others, owe him a great debt ... [he has helped me] to broaden and deepen my understanding of the meaning and the requisites of a free society. ❞
>
> Milton Friedman, foreword in Fritz Machlup, *Essays on Hayek*

interventions in the economy could be used as instruments of power for particular groups in society. This transformation of democratic institutions into servants of particular interest groups, Hayek believed, would empower such groups and lead to the erosion of democracy.

Adaptations of Hayek's ideas such as the formulation of public choice theory led people to rethink the need for a public sector, and indirectly led to increased privatization* of industries previously owned by the government. They also led to the reform of the public sector, first in the western world and then, after the end of the Cold War,* in much of the rest of the world. Hayek's ideas provided an alternative to political socialism and to the idea of the large state as a goal in itself. They also contributed to a change in how people saw the role of government.

Achievement In Context

In 1945, despite paper being scarce, the British Conservative Party* used its supply "so that abridged copies [of *The Road to Serfdom*] could be printed as campaign literature."[2] By the 1960s, Hayek's ideas were considered outmoded, with the British political philosopher Anthony Quinton* describing him as a "magnificent dinosaur."[3] Since the

1970s, Hayek and his book have experienced a renaissance that has lasted until the present day. The book is still regarded as relevant in terms of its political importance, its ability to attract supporters of views shared by Hayek, and its status as a source of controversial economic history.

Conservatives in many different political situations refer to the book, especially when they want to oppose liberal policies that increase the government's role in the economy. When Chicago economist Milton Friedman* wrote the introduction to the 50th-anniversary edition of the book in 1994, he declared that "we badly need a new book ... that will give as clear and penetrating insight into the intellectual developments of the past quarter century as *The Road to Serfdom* does of earlier developments."[4] The book is now seen even more as an ideological inspiration because it has been the center of so much debate. In 2012 it featured in a bbc documentary about Hayek, and *Time* magazine cited it as one of the works that former Republican vice-presidential nominee Paul Ryan* regularly re-reads.[5]

Limitations

The Road to Serfdom has a certain limitation as a political book rooted in the context of the period between World War I* and World War II.* Hayek wrote from his own experience in 1920s and 1930s Vienna and from what he had read about Nazi Germany* and the Soviet Union.* This makes the book difficult to understand if you are not familiar with the period. Its ideas are also hard to apply in a non-European, non-American or modern context and demand a broad knowledge of European history, philosophy and economic research.

To understand its social context, the reader must know about Hayek's upbringing, the period when his interest in philosophy, law, psychology and economics began. These were the subjects he would write about in *The Road to Serfdom*. It is also important to know that, unlike many in his generation, Hayek spent time as a visiting scholar in the United States before returning to Austria. This meant he had already experienced Anglo-Saxon culture before he moved to London.

The reader should also take into account the fact that Hayek witnessed the rise of communism* in Russia and that of fascism* and Nazism* in Italy, Austria and Germany. This convinced him of the similarities between all three ideologies.

Finally, we need to look at the cultural context to fully understand the work as a whole. Hayek saw the German culture of including the state in all aspects of the life of the individual as potentially representing the beginning of a totalitarian state.* He contrasted this "idea of a political party which embraces all activities of the individual from the cradle to the grave"[6] with the idea of Anglo-Saxon individualism, politically translated into economic liberalism.* The difference between the two needs to be understood if a reader is to grasp one of the book's most important themes.

NOTES

1   Peter J. Boettke and Peter T. Leeson, "An 'Austrian' Perspective on Public Choice," in *Encyclopedia of Public Choice*, eds Charles K. Rowley and Friedrich Schneider (Boston, MA: Kluwer, 2003).

2   David Willetts, "The New Conservatism? 1945–1951," in *Recovering Power: The Conservatives in Opposition since 1867*, eds Stuart Ball and Anthony Seldon (Basingstoke: Palgrave Macmillan, 2005), 171.

3   Anthony Quinton, ed., *Political Philosophy* (Oxford: Oxford University Press, 1967), 2.

4   Milton Friedman, "Introduction to the 1994 Edition," in F. A. Hayek, *The Road to Serfdom: Texts and Documents – The Definitive Edition*, ed. Bruce Caldwell (Chicago, IL: Chicago University Press, 2008), 262.

5   Michael Crowley, "The Big Idea Guy," *Time Magazine*, September 3, 2012, http://www.content.time.com/time/magazine/article/0,9171,2122768,00. html, accessed January 24, 2014.

6   F. A. Hayek, *The Road to Serfdom: Texts and Documents – The Definitive Edition*, ed. Bruce Caldwell (Chicago, IL: Chicago University Press, 2008), 144.

MODULE 8
PLACE IN THE AUTHOR'S WORK

KEY POINTS

- *The Road to Serfdom* is closely related to Hayek's other academic works, though it would be an overstatement to say it is a distillation of his life's work.

- Like Hayek's entire career, this book is closely associated with the principles of the Austrian School of Economics, with its emphasis on the importance of individual behavior rather than social structures.

- Hayek's contribution to "linking economic, social and institutional phenomena" was rewarded in 1974, when he was jointly (with Gunnar Myrdal) awarded the Nobel Memorial Prize in Economic Sciences.

Positioning

The Road to Serfdom is the first attempt by Friedrich Hayek to express a coherent political argument rather than an economic one. Yet it also builds on his previous works criticizing socialism,* so it is a logical progression. It is not, however, a distillation of a lifetime's work, but the first thing the author contributed to the debate as a political philosopher.[1] Hayek's career lasted from the 1920s to the 1980s, but it was only after he wrote *The Road to Serfdom* that he became "Hayek the thinker" rather than "Hayek the economist" in public debate. The book also anticipated later writings such as *The Constitution of Liberty* (1960) and *The Fatal Conceit* (1988), which laid out reasons why intellectuals were often attracted to socialism.

The Road to Serfdom came about before Hayek made efforts to construct a system that would maximize freedom in society. In this

> 66 Hayek, in my view, is the leading economic thinker of the twentieth century 99
>
> Vernon Smith, Nobel Prize-winning economist, "Reflections on Human Action after 50 Years"

book, though, he was already starting to form ideas about what he called "spontaneous order." As he explained: "The fundamental principle that in the ordering of our affairs we should make as much use as possible of the spontaneous forces of society, and resort as little as possible to coercion, is capable of an infinite variety of application."[2] His work is intellectually consistent, but it is not simply a presentation of new ideas—rather, it is an argument against popular ideas expressed at the time. Hayek also thought of adding a postscript to the book after the Labour Party* won the British general election in 1945, exploring how this would change the political landscape. But he eventually abandoned the idea.

Integration

Hayek's intellectual thinking took in many ideas, but it united around the core ideas of the Austrian School of Economics, where Hayek was a leading figure. According to the economist Peter Boettke, one of the key characteristics of the Austrian School is the idea that "social institutions are often the result of human action, but not of human design."[3] For example, in his 1948 book *Individualism and Economic Order*, Hayek tells a story of a student walking through snow. This student cuts across the snowy lawn to get to class sooner, and the footprints he leaves encourage others to follow. Eventually, a path has formed that all students can use to cross the lawn. The path didn't happen because someone had planned it—it developed organically from the first student's impulsive decision. Hayek calls this "path in the snow" story a simple example of a "product of human action, but not of design."[4] With this in mind, it is possible to see how Hayek's criticism of socialism* may have emerged from a similar seed. Hayek's view of planning is that too much design inhibits the natural flow of economic life.

Hayek's skepticism* about scientific knowledge, particularly when it is applied to social matters, relates indirectly to *The Road to Serfdom.* According to Peter Boettke, another of the beliefs of the Austrian School is that "the 'facts' of the social sciences are what people believe and think," rather than objective truth.[5] In his 1974 Nobel Prize lecture, Hayek addressed what he called the "pretense of knowledge." He was talking in particular about the difficulty of inferring anything about policy outcomes from studying economic data. In the social sciences, only some aspects of a complicated process can be turned into quantitative data. Take the example of the relationship between aggregate demand—the total demand of a given society—and unemployment. The data we have only tell part of the story. As Hayek writes: "The correlation between aggregate demand and total employment, for instance, may only be approximate, but as it is the *only* one on which we have quantitative data, it is accepted as the only causal connection that counts."[6] In other words, there may be many "aggregate demands" in reality, but we are only able to observe one, so therefore our conclusions are as uncertain as that data point.

Hayek is uncertain about the relationship between economic knowledge and policy outcomes and this is why he challenges the whole idea of planning in the first place. His criticism of planning is that it assumes the economic planner knows more than he actually does and so gives him more authority than he truly merits.

Significance

The Road to Serfdom established Hayek as "the world's leading classic liberal."[7] If they know anything at all about Hayek, most people who are not economists would most likely think of *The Road to Serfdom* in connection with him, as is by far Hayek's most widely read work. Economists, however, see this book as just one of many of his influential works. When Hayek was awarded a Nobel Prize in 1974, it was for his "penetrating analysis of the interdependence of economic, social and institutional phenomena." These topics all play an important role in *The Road to Serfdom*, but they also appear throughout his work.[8] If it weren't for his extensive writing on knowledge in society and his important contributions to the debates on monetary policy and economic fluctuations, Hayek would be far less influential.

Hayek's critique of socialism included the important idea that central planners could not possibly have to hand all the information about the economy that was necessary to make sound decisions. This idea has been so widely embraced among economists that it is now almost considered common sense. Jeffrey Sachs,* for example, noted how economists were often unable to identify sound investments: "If you ask an economist where's a good place to invest, which industries are going to grow, where the specialization is going to occur, the track record is pretty miserable. Economists don't collect the on-the-ground information businessmen do. Every time Poland asks, Well, what are we going to be able to produce? I say I don't know."[9]

NOTES

1 Alan Ebenstein, *Friedrich Hayek: A Biography* (New York: Palgrave Macmillan, 2001).

2 F. A. Hayek, *The Road to Serfdom: Texts and Documents – The Definitive Edition*, ed. Bruce Caldwell (Chicago, IL: Chicago University Press, 2008), 71.

3 Peter Boettke, "Austrian School of Economics," *Library of Economics and Liberty*, http://www.econlib.org/library/Enc/AustrianSchoolofEconomics.html, accessed March 5, 2015.

4 F. A. Hayek, *Individualism and Economic Order* (Chicago: University of Chicago Press, 1948), 7.

5   Boettke, "Austrian School."

6   F.A. Hayek, "Prize Lecture: The Pretense of Knowledge," http://www.
     nobelprize.org/nobel_prizes/economic-sciences/laureates/1974/hayek-
     lecture.html, accessed March 6, 2015.

7   "Friedrich August Hayek," Library of Economics and Liberty, http://www.
     econlib.org/library/Enc/bios/Hayek.html, accessed March 8, 2015.

8   "Friedrich August von Hayek - Facts". *Nobelprize.org*. Nobel Media AB 2014,
     http://www.nobelprize.org/nobel_prizes/economic-sciences/laureates/1974/
     hayek-facts.html, accessed March 8, 2015.

9   "Interview: Jeffrey Sachs," *Omni* 13, no. 9 (1991), 79.

SECTION 3
IMPACT

MODULE 9
THE FIRST RESPONSES

KEY POINTS

- Early criticisms of *The Road to Serfdom* rejected Hayek's claim that planning and freedom are incompatible.
- There were more negative reactions to the book in the United States than in Europe. In Hayek's view, this was because Americans were less familiar with the dangers of economic planning.
- Hayek made no changes to the ideas in his book in subsequent editions and did not try to appease his critics.

Criticism

The main aspect of *The Road to Serfdom* that attracted criticism was Friedrich Hayek's suggestion that increased economic planning* would lead to a situation where society has "abandoned that freedom in economic affairs without which personal and political freedom has never existed in the past."[1] In her book *Freedom Under Planning*, the sociologist Barbara Wootton argued that "there is nothing in the conscious planning of economic priorities which is inherently incompatible with the freedoms which mean most to the contemporary Englishman or American. Civil liberties are quite unaffected. We can, if we wish, deliberately plan so as to give the fullest possible scope for the pursuit by individuals and social groups of cultural ends which are in no way state-determined."[2]

A more heated attack came from the socialist Herman Finer,* who, in his book *The Road to Reaction*, attempted to show that "Hayek's apparatus of learning is deficient, his reading incomplete; that his understanding of the economic process is bigoted, his account of

> **❝** *The Road to Serfdom* was a popular success but was not a good book. Leaving aside the irrelevant extremes, or even including them, it would be perverse to read the history, as of 1944 or as of now, as suggesting that the standard regulatory interventions in the economy have any inherent tendency to snowball into 'serfdom.'**❞**
>
> Robert Solow, *Hayek, Friedman, and the Illusions of Conservative Economics*

history false … and that his attitude to average men and women is truculently authoritarian."[3]

Another critique argued that *The Road to Serfdom* was not a work of economics at all. When the book was about to be published in the United States, a reader's report by the University of Chicago economist Frank Knight said that the non-economic chapters were open to criticism on "the ground of over-simplification" and that the book was "limited in scope."[4] Knight also attacked Hayek's treatment of the government's role in the economy, saying that he "inadequately recognizes the necessity, as well as political inevitability, of a wide range of governmental activity in relation to economic life in the future."[5]

Responses

Hayek was prepared for criticism of his book, but he was not prepared for the extent of the criticism. After *The Road to Serfdom* was published in 1944, his London School of Economics* colleague Harold Laski* "believed it was a book written especially against him" and stopped speaking to Hayek.[6]

Hayek welcomed criticism he thought was fair and directed at the book. He believed that "the English socialists, with few exceptions, accepted the book as something written in good faith, raising problems they were willing to consider."[7] The debate heated up, however, when the book was published in the United States. Hayek thought he was "exposed to incredible abuse … It went so far as to completely discredit me professionally."[8] An example of this was Finer's 1945 book *The Road to Reaction*. According to Hayek, American hostility was due to "the new enthusiasm of all the New Dealers," who supported President Franklin D. Roosevelt's positive government action to try to fix a failing economy via public building works and increased government action. According to Hayek, the less hostile reaction to the book in Britain was because it had been published there "at a stage where people had already become aware of the dangers of socialism."[9]

Hayek did not get into a dialogue with his opponents, but when he travelled to the United States for a book tour in 1945 he took part in several public debates. Many critics said *The Road to Serfdom* was a work of party politics. Hayek replied that he was not for or against any political party; it was simply against governmental planning.* In a radio debate he emphasized that he was "a convinced free trader," which meant he was also against tariffs* and the idea that government should support or bail out companies in difficulty.[10]

In the foreword to the 1956 American paperback edition of *The Road to Serfdom*, Hayek said that he was surprised "by the lavish praise the book received from some quarters no less than by the passionate hatred it appeared to arouse in others."[11] His American opponents saw him as a defender of circumstances that had led to economic depression and mass unemployment in the 1930s. Hayek did not revise the important content of the book for the American editions. An original reader's report for the American market had complained that the book was written from a "distinctly English point of view" that "might limit the appeal."[12] The only changes Hayek made were in small details, such as writing "Britain" when he had previously referred to "this country."

Conflict And Consensus

While most people were in favor of economic planning when the book was first published, this generally held view was undermined by the debate sparked by *The Road to Serfdom*. Hayek's initial ambition was to transform opinion in the British Liberal Party,* but he actually succeeded in doing so among members of the country's Conservative Party*. In the words of British political historian Richard Cockett, the book "reorientated the political discourse within the Party along an individualist–collectivist axis, thus laying the parameters for a post-war debate within the party."[13] What Cockett meant was that *The Road to Serfdom* had set the debate along the lines of the benefits of the individual versus those of the collective group. It also gave a voice to broader anti-collectivist* feelings, which led to the foundation and work of the Institute of Economic Affairs* in London.

All this debate around *The Road to Serfdom* most likely strengthened the book. First of all, it enabled its criticisms of government planning to be heard by a wide general public. Second, it allowed these ideas to become influential in a major British political party—the Conservatives. Third, Hayek achieved his aim of convincing individuals that they should invest both time and resources in resisting government planning.

Hayek's views became influential in the decades that followed the book's publication. The work of those who criticized him, however, did not. Hayek did not make any changes to *The Road to Serfdom* on the basis of the criticism he received, and therefore we can conclude that his ideas became more dominant than those of anyone who tried to counter them.

NOTES

1   F. A. Hayek, *The Road to Serfdom: Texts and Documents – The Definitive Edition*, ed. Bruce Caldwell (Chicago, IL: Chicago University Press, 2008), 67.

2   Barbara Wootton, *Freedom Under Planning* (Chapel Hill: University of North Carolina Press, 1945), 158.

3   Herman Finer, *The Road to Reaction* (Boston: Little Brown and Company, 1945), Preface.

4   Frank Knight, "Reader's Report," in Hayek, *The Road to Serfdom*, 250.

5   Knight, "Reader's Report," 251.

6   Alan Ebenstein, *Friedrich Hayek: A Biography* (New York: Palgrave Macmillan, 2001), 56.

7   F. A. Hayek, *Hayek on Hayek: An Autobiographical Dialogue – The Collected Works of F. A. Hayek*, ed. Stephen Kresge and Leif Wenar (London: Routledge, 1994), 102.

8   Hayek, *Hayek on Hayek*, 102–3.

9   Hayek, *Hayek on Hayek*, 104.

10 Hayek, *Hayek on Hayek*, 115.

11 F.A. Hayek, "Foreword to the 1956 American Paperback Edition," in Hayek, *The Road to Serfdom*, 41.

12 Frank Knight in Hayek, *The Road to Serfdom*, 249.

13 Richard Cockett, *Thinking the Unthinkable: Think Tanks and the Economic Counter-Revolution, 1931–1983* (London: HarperCollins, 1994), 97.

MODULE 10
THE EVOLVING DEBATE

KEY POINTS

- *The Road to Serfdom* started a move in economic research towards fighting inflation where it had previously focused on fighting unemployment.

- The work is associated with the liberal or neo-liberal school in economics, which is in favor of a small state structure and as little interference in the economy as possible.

- Modern thinkers who admire Hayek use the book to illustrate their concerns about the dominating power of institutions such as the European Union (EU).*

Uses And Problems

It is hard to overstate the importance of Friedrich Hayek's *The Road to Serfdom*, both in public debate and in the evolution of economics. The book played a part in the British general election campaign of 1945 when it was talked about by Prime Minister Sir Winston Churchill,* and it effectively reintroduced the idea of classical liberalism* into British political debate. It also helped to reignite the study of economic liberalism* as Hayek himself established the Mont Pelerin Society,* an international group of academics who were invited "to discuss the state and possible fate of liberalism."[1] The society's first meeting was held in 1947 in Switzerland, and before the conference got under way, Hayek outlined the society's aims in a memo. According to him, the society existed because if Europe were not to enter a "new kind of serfdom, an intense intellectual effort is needed."[2] Since its foundation, besides Hayek himself, the society has had seven Nobel laureates as members.

> ❝ Hayek's powerful *Road to Serfdom* left a permanent mark on my own political character, making me a long-term optimist for free enterprise and liberty. ❞
>
> Margaret Thatcher, *The Downing Street Years*

The most important practical economic effect of *The Road to Serfdom* was that it started a shift in research from fighting unemployment—as John Maynard Keynes* proposed— to fighting inflation instead. This was not an idea that was concretely suggested in the book, but it was alluded to when Hayek attacked the idea of economic planning.* "If we are determined not to allow unemployment at any price, and are not willing to use coercion, we shall be driven to all sorts of desperate expedients," he warned.[3]

The text has also fuelled a wider intellectual debate, because Hayek's work in many ways reflected the thinking of the Austrian School of Economics,* which also influenced the Chicago School of Economics. Both schools were behind the idea of fighting inflation by controlling the supply of money, rather than by reducing unemployment. The us government embraced this approach during the presidency of Ronald Reagan* at the same time as the book was having a major influence on the British government led by Margaret Thatcher.*

After Hayek's death in 1992, the book also had an impact in those formerly communist* countries that had once been behind the Iron Curtain*. Czech Republic President Václav Havel* contemplated the idea that the country's new senate should be based on "Friedrich Hayek's idea of a division of functions."[4] The book also contributed to the common belief that socialism* was incompatible with maintaining democracy* and private ownership.

Schools Of Thought

The Road to Serfdom has inspired many different writers and thinkers. These include British Prime Minister Sir Winston Churchill* and the founder of the Institute of Economic Affairs,* Sir Antony Fisher. American Senator Barry Goldwater*—the 1964 Republican Presidential candidate against Lyndon Johnson*—named Thomas Jefferson as his favorite president and Friedrich Hayek as his favorite political philosopher.[5] Many have argued that Goldwater's 1964 book *The Conscience of a Conservative* built on the argument introduced by Hayek in *The Road to Serfdom* that the duty of government is to safeguard freedom. Goldwater's disciples included future presidents Ronald Reagan* and George H.W. Bush.* Both were also influenced by Hayek.

The school of thought that formed around these ideas could be characterized as favoring liberal or neo-liberal* economics. This is an approach that advocates a small state structure and as little interference in the economy as possible. Politically, this school of thought was most clearly represented by Reagan and British Prime Minister Margaret Thatcher.* Neo-liberals adopted the ideas in *The Road to Serfdom*, while both customizing and modernizing them. In 1983 American Republican congressman and Hayek supporter Newt Gingrich suggested to Reagan that he should freeze the budget in order to reduce the budget deficit, which at the time was growing. In his diary Reagan described the plan to freeze the budget as "a tempting idea except that it would cripple our defense program." Reagan adapted Hayek's proposal for a smaller government to make it fit with the geo-political* problems he was facing in the context of the Cold War.*[6]

Hayek's supporters modernized his ideas by suggesting that a system of government welfare should be organized in such a way that it demanded something in return from those who received that welfare. Ideas like these were of interest both to the British Conservative* governments under prime ministers Thatcher and

John Major*, and also to the New Democrats* in the United States. There were also traces of this thinking in the Big Society* philosophy proposed by the Conservative–Liberal Democrat coalition government that was in power in the UK until May 2015. In the spirit of Hayek, that coalition's manifesto claimed: "Our government will be a much smarter one, shunning the bureaucratic levers of the past and finding intelligent ways to encourage, support, and enable people to make better choices for themselves."[7]

In Current Scholarship

Current supporters of *The Road to Serfdom* believe the powers of the state can still be excessive and therefore also dangerous. The book does not anticipate modern events such as the "War on Terror,"* but modern supporters would think of the American-led anti-"terrorist" actions throughout the Middle East to which that term refers as a perfect expression of the totalitarian* tendencies Hayek was warning against. They say this danger has shown itself in a number of ways—in excessive taxation, in excessively harsh legislation,* and in international federalism,* particularly with regard to the powers of the EU. *The Road to Serfdom* fits into the belief system of those who favor a small state with limited powers. Such people also agree with international cooperation, but only to the extent that it enhances free trade. It would be possible to argue that modern disciples of the book are highly critical of the eu, which they see as an international organization with excessive powers. Supporters of Hayek therefore make use of the book by applying his fear about excessive government power to a modern context.

Whether Hayek's followers have managed to convince people of the truth of his arguments is hard to say right now. The success of Hayek's ideas could have been greatly increased by a Republican* win in the US presidential elections of 2012. However, it could also be argued that Hayek's modern following has greatly increased with the birth in 2009 of the US Tea Party movement,* which advocates public spending cuts and a reduction in the size of the US government.

NOTES

1 "About MPS," The Mont Pelerin Society website, https://www.montpelerin.org/montpelerin/mpsAbout.html, accessed January 25, 2014.

2 Cited in Alan Ebenstein, *Friedrich Hayek: A Biography* (New York: Palgrave Macmillan, 2001), 143.

3 F. A. Hayek, *The Road to Serfdom: Texts and Documents – The Definitive Edition*, ed. Bruce Caldwell (Chicago, IL: Chicago University Press, 2008), 214.

4 Václav Havel, *To the Castle and Back* (London: Portobello, 2008), 180.

5 Lee Edwards, *Goldwater* (Washington, DC: Regnery, 1995), 281.

6 Ronald Reagan, *The Reagan Diaries*, ed. Douglas Brinkley (New York: HarperCollins, 2007), 123.

7 "The Coalition: Our Programme for Government," https://www.gov.uk/government/uploads/system/uploads/attachment_data/file/78977/coalition_programme_for_government.pdf, accessed March 8, 2015.

IMPACT AND INFLUENCE TODAY

KEY POINTS

- Both *The Road to Serfdom* and John Maynard Keynes's* *General Theory of Employment, Interest and Money* were consulted as economic guides for how to approach the 2007–8 financial crisis.*

- Some people believed that British New Labour* in the 1990s accepted Hayek's view that equality was not desirable.

- In the aftermath of the financial crisis, some have put forward the idea that greater equality benefits society as a whole.

Position

Friedrich Hayek's *The Road to Serfdom* is still relevant today in a number of different ways. Together with John Maynard Keynes's *The General Theory of Employment, Interest and Money*, it has been widely read in recent times as a kind of guidebook to where contemporary economics is, and where it fits into the world of politics. Modern economics in the public arena revolves around spending, or spending cuts, and an understanding of *The Road to Serfdom* is essential for understanding how this issue evolved in a historical sense.

From the economic crisis of 2007–8 onwards, many ways of thinking about economic policy-making can be traced back either to Keynes or to Hayek. For example, the British Chancellor of the Exchequer at the time of the crisis, Alistair Darling,* at first thought that "the Keynesian approach would prevail" as a response to the crisis,

> **"** Socialism is a philosophy of failure, the creed of ignorance, and the gospel of envy, its inherent virtue is the equal sharing of misery. **"**
> Sir Winston Churchill, in a speech

and that governments would intervene to get things back to normal. But as he later acknowledged in his memoirs, "in Europe there followed a reaction, both political and economic, that owed much more to Hayek than to Keynes."[1] This interpretation of Hayek is captured in Nicholas Wapshott's 2011 work *Keynes–Hayek: The Clash that Defined Modern Economics*. In a review of the book, Hayek's views were explained as "upholding a pure free-market doctrine, in which economic salvation comes through faith, not works—and especially not public works."[2] Hayek's work has clearly been revived in current political debate.

Yet the views of modern supporters of *The Road to Serfdom* often clash with the original intentions of the book. Such people tend to be professed neo-conservatives* or conservatives,* while Hayek never saw himself as a conservative and even objected to being called one. Although Hayek originally intended his book to be a work of liberal ideology, it has been transformed into a work of conservative ideology, which throws up several challenges when it comes to understanding the work in the context of today's world, while still remaining true to its original spirit.

Interaction

The Road to Serfdom still poses a challenge to socialism* and social democracy,* as well as to Keynesian economics.* When in the 1990s British Labour politician Peter Mandelson* declared that New Labour* was "intensely relaxed about people getting filthy rich," his comments could be interpreted as an acceptance of Hayek's idea that equality was not a desirable goal.[3] In this way—and as *The Road to Serfdom* said—the left "accepted the imperfection of the market, since economic activity took place between consumers with imperfect knowledge."[4]

The book was also used to challenge communist* ideology during the Cold War,* and still does so where such thinking still exists today. It was reprinted in several countries during the Cold-War period and understandably had a major renaissance after Hayek was jointly awarded the Nobel Memorial Prize in Economic Sciences in 1974. The University of Chicago Press, which published the book in the United States, estimated that between 1944 and 1994 the book sold over a quarter of a million copies.[5] There were also illegal printings of the book from behind the Iron Curtain* during the Cold War. In the words of economist Milton Friedman,* "there is little doubt that Hayek's writings, and especially this book, were an important intellectual source of the disintegration of faith in communism behind the Iron Curtain."[6]

The Continuing Debate

The ideas presented in *The Road to Serfdom* came to dominate between the end of the Cold War and the economic crisis of 2007–8.* However, in the light of the crisis, the text's basic ideas were challenged. In 2009, *The Spirit Level: Why Equality is Better for Everyone* by Richard G. Wilkinson and Kate Pickett argued that equality was economically beneficial to society as a whole. This was an intellectual attempt to go against the general idea proposed by Hayek that trying to establish equality can be dangerous for society because it threatens democracy.

The revival of political Keynesianism—the idea that the government should intervene in difficult economic times—can also be seen as a response to Hayek's ideas. Keynes's biographer, the historian Robert Skidelsky, claimed that "except for Hayekian fanatics, it seems obvious that the coordinated global stimulus of 2009 stopped the slide into another Great Depression."[7] Skidelsky was referring to the fact that governments did indeed interfere in their economies— by bailing out banks and approving significant fiscal stimulus packages—to avert an even greater disaster.

Skidelsky's was not so much a direct, coordinated attack on Hayek as a series of spontaneous responses to the economic crisis. The motives behind the responses can be divided into intellectual, professional, personal, and political. Supporters of a larger state saw the crisis as a way to question the core of Hayek's argument from a philosophical point of view. There were professional and personal motives in the case of Skidelsky, much of whose work focuses on Keynes. Additionally, there were political motives among socialists and social democrats* who wanted to use the crisis to gain credibility for their political beliefs.

NOTES

1   Alistair Darling, *Back from the Brink: 1000 Days at Number 11* (London: Atlantic Books, 2011), xviii.

2   Peter Clarke, "Keynes–Hayek by Nicholas Wapshott – Review," *Guardian*, February 3, 2012, http://www.theguardian.com/books/2012/feb/03/keynes-hayek-nicholas-wapshott-review, accessed January 24, 2014.

3   Steve Hart, "Equality Must Be at the Centre of a Vision for a Better Society," *New Statesman*, September 11, 2012, http://www.newstatesman.com/blogs/economics/2012/09/equality-must-be-centre-vision-better-society, accessed January 24, 2014.

4   Kevin Hickson, "Economic Thought," in *New Labour, Old Labour: The Wilson and Callaghan Governments, 1974–79*, ed. Anthony Seldon and Kevin Hickson (London: Routledge, 2004), 36.

5   Milton Friedman, "Introduction to the 1994 Edition," in F. A. Hayek, *The Road to Serfdom: Texts and Documents – The Definitive Edition*, ed. Bruce Caldwell (Chicago, IL: Chicago University Press, 2008), 264.

6   Friedman, "Introduction to the 1994 Edition," 264.

7   Robert Skidelsky, "The Keynes–Hayek Rematch," Project Syndicate, August 19, 2011, http://www.project-syndicate.org/commentary/the-keynes-hayek-

MODULE 12
WHERE NEXT?

KEY POINTS

- *The Road to Serfdom* will probably continue to sound an important warning against excessive government control. How seriously that warning will be taken will likely ebb and flow over time.

- The book will continue to have academic impact as the Austrian School of Economics, from where much of Hayek's thinking developed, remains important in graduate study.

- Friedrich Hayek's *The Road to Serfdom* is a foundational book in economics due to the boldness of its claim that socialism* will lead to similar outcomes to fascism,* and because many of the ideas in the book have been important in political policymaking.

Potential

What the future holds for Friedrich Hayek's *The Road to Serfdom* can likely be divided into three different scenarios. The first is one in which the book is used to inspire resistance every time there are politicians who suggest more government planning* and increased government control. Since its original publication in 1944, successive generations have rediscovered the book, and this looks likely to continue. The second scenario is one where the book's reputation suffers because of the economic crisis that began in 2007–8.* This crisis severely damaged the public's faith in free-market* systems, and this disenchantment will probably linger. The third scenario is a mixture of the two, whereby the book's critics see the book as being out of fashion, but a text that would become popular again when

> **❝** While in graduate school I encountered the writings of Friedrich Hayek and Ludwig von Mises, which shook me out of my then socialist beliefs. **❞**
>
> Robert Nozick, *The Harvard Guide to Influential Books*

politicians start to propose excessive government planning.

It is also possible to imagine how the book's core ideas might develop. The notion that economic planning is dangerous for democracy* and might eventually lead to the introduction of totalitarianism* could be detected in the debate about the introduction of universal health care insurance in the United States. As a 2013 report from the conservative American Enterprise Institute* stated in response to one of US President Barack Obama's* public speeches on the subject: "The entire Obama press conference today played out like some Hayekian cautionary tale where a befuddled central planner complains about the complexity of real life."[1]

A second core idea about planning and international relations can be seen in the ongoing debate about the future of the European Union.* This has been portrayed as a clash between those who want to see a federal* union and those who prefer a union between free-trading nation states. Hayek expressed a preference for the latter structure, and anticipated this exchange in *The Road to Serfdom*.

Future Directions
In the future, it looks likely that Hayek's ideas will be tied to the study and application of ideas from the Austrian School of Economics. In the United States, one of the key intellectual hubs of Austrian theory is George Mason University (GMU), which offers an "F. A. Hayek Program for Advanced Study in Philosophy, Economics, and Politics."[2] Peter Boettke, a professor at GMU, suggests that the future of Austrian work will depend on following the example of the school's founders:

"My message to graduate students is to learn from Mises* and Hayek in the way that they approached their research and teaching in economics and political economy. And that means ... your goal in writing papers should be to adopt arguments and make them your own and develop them in your unique intellectual context and engage your peers."³

In the spirit of Boettke's statement, the future of Hayek's ideas depends on scholars developing bold ideas that engage active debate across a broad community. One possible candidate to carry out this work is Christopher Coyne, a professor at GMU whose work on institutions and entrepreneurship won him the Atlas Economic Research Foundation's Hayek Prize in 2007.

Summary

The Road to Serfdom is significant both intellectually and historically. The fact that it is still read by influential policymakers and economists shows that it is still relevant.

Anyone reading *The Road to Serfdom* will start to appreciate the complexity of some of the most important questions in economics and politics—namely:

- How should society be organized?
- How can individual freedom be protected?
- What balance must societies find between equality and liberty?

Though Hayek's approach to these questions is certainly a product of his time, the questions themselves are still hugely important in modern-day public debate and conversation. In most societies, the question of how public resources should be allocated is at the very center of political debate, and *The Road to Serfdom* is one of the best introductions to the view that economic freedoms must be protected, even if the cost must be inequality.

Readers of *The Road to Serfdom* will also develop intellectual skills that can be applied beyond a historical understanding of the structure of the economy. They will develop debating and arguing skills regardless of their political persuasion. Those who support socialist programs may have the most to gain from reading the book, because it will force them to challenge their own beliefs and develop arguments to defend their views. But critics of socialism also have plenty to gain from reading *The Road to Serfdom*, because they will be exposed to Hayek's radical viewpoint, which may again challenge or even change some of their most deeply held convictions

NOTES

1   James Pethokoukis, "Obamacare, Meet Hayek," *American Enterprise Institute*, http://www.aei.org/publication/obamacare-meet-hayek/, accessed March 8, 2015.

2   "Mercatus Center," http://ppe.mercatus.org/, accessed March 8, 2015.

3   Peter Boettke, "Teaching Austrian Economics to Graduate Students," *Journal of Economics and Finance Education* 10, no. 2 (2011): 22.

GLOSSARY

GLOSSARY OF TERMS

Allies: the collective name given to the group of nations, including Great Britain, the Soviet Union and the United States, that fought the Axis powers of Germany, Italy and Japan in World War II, the global conflict that took place between 1939 and 1945.

American Enterprise Institute: an American public policy think tank dedicated to researching issues related to governance, economics, and social welfare from a conservative, free-enterprise perspective.

Beveridge Report: the informal name of the report 'Social Insurance and Allied Services (1942)'. It was written by William Beveridge, a British economist and social reformer, and proposed the welfare strategy that was later followed by the British Labour Party from 1945 until 1951.

Big Society: a philosophy articulated by the British political philosopher Philip Blond (born 1966) in his book *Red Tory: How Left and Right Have Broken Britain and How We Can Fix It* (London: Faber, 2010). It focuses on the idea that citizens should play a greater part in the running of public institutions such as schools and libraries. It was a core part of the British Conservative Party's election campaign in 2010.

British Liberal Party: one of the major political parties in Britain. In 1988, it merged with the Social Democratic Party to form the Social and Liberal Democrats, renamed the Liberal Democrats in 1989.

Capitalism: an economic system based on private ownership, private enterprise and the maximization of profit.

Central planning: when the government exercises direct ownership and control over a nation's economy, rather than leaving it to the free market.

Classical liberalism: a political philosophy and ideology that emerged in Europe and the United States in the nineteenth century in response to industrialization and urbanization. It supports the protection of individual liberties and a limited government.

Cold War: a long period of tension and enmity between Eastern and Western powers and, in particular, between the Soviet Union and the United States, usually dated from 1947 to 1991.

Collectivism: a social and economic perspective that emphasizes the interrelatedness of all human beings. It is often presented in contrast to individualism, which highlights independence or self-reliance of individuals.

Communism: a political and economic doctrine that rejects private ownership and advocates that all property should be vested in the community for the benefit of all.

Conservative Party: center-right political party in the United Kingdom, often referred to as the Tory Party. Conservatives tend to support free enterprise and individual liberty.

Democracy: a system of government in which the people exercise power, either directly or through elected representatives.

Depression: a severe and prolonged downturn in a country's economic output. Technically, depressions are often defined as either a 10 percent decline in national output or any downturn lasting more than two years.

Dictatorship: a political regime in which authority is held by a single individual or political entity.

European Union: an economic and political union established in 1993 through the Treaty of Maastricht. It built on the European Economic Community, which was established by the Treaty of Rome in 1957. The EU reached its current size of 28 member countries with the accession of Croatia on July 1, 2013.

Fascism: a dictatorship that is characterized by strict political, economic, and social controls, and which disallows any form of opposition to the government.

Federalism: a political concept in which power is shared between political entities but organized around a single federal authority. The United States and the European Union are examples of federalist systems.

Federal Stimulus Package: also known as the American Recovery and Reinvestment Act of 2009, this was a bill authorizing more than $800 billion in spending, split between tax cuts and spending on governmental programs, designed to increase economic growth in the United States. The bill was inspired by Keynesian economic principles.

Financial crisis of 2007–8: an economic crisis that originated in the United States housing market and spread through much of Europe and beyond. It is considered to be the most significant financial crisis since the Great Depression of the 1930s. Major banks and other financial institutions collapsed and economic activity slumped. Huge government bailouts prevented even greater disaster.

Free markets: an economic system in which goods and services are exchanged in markets and where prices are set by the interaction between supply and demand rather than by the government.

Geo-political: the combination of geographical, economic, and political factors influencing a country and its approach to international relations.

Great Depression: a significant global economic downturn in the years 1929–39.

Institute of Economic Affairs: a free-market think tank established in 1955 by Sir Antony Fisher and Arthur Seldon.

International Monetary Fund: an organization of 188 countries, based in Washington, DC, that promotes global financial stability. It lends money to heavily indebted countries when no one else will.

Iron Curtain: a phrase popularized by Sir Winston Churchill, referring to the post-war division between communist Eastern Europe and capitalist Western Europe.

Keynesian economics: when the government spends money in order to tackle unemployment.

Labour Party: a center-left political party in the United Kingdom.

League of Nations (1920–46): an international organization founded in the aftermath of World War I. It is considered to be the precursor to the modern United Nations.

Legislation: law that has been enacted by a legislature—for example, the British Parliament or the United States Senate. Legislation typically has the purpose of regulating, authorizing, restricting, or granting particular behaviors.

Liberal Party: a political party in the United Kingdom formed from several earlier parties (including the Whigs, the Radicals, and the Peelites). Notably, the Liberals introduced a number of reforms that created the British "welfare state."

Liberalism: a political philosophy that emphasizes freedom, equality, and regularly contested elections.

London School of Economics: a public research university in the United Kingdom specializing in many aspects of the social sciences, particularly economics and political science.

Monetarism: an economic philosophy, developed mainly at the University of Chicago, which argued that the most important task governments have is to prevent inflation. This could be achieved by reducing the supply of money in the economy.

Mont Pelerin Society: an international economic think tank dedicated to studying and promoting individual freedom. Notable economists such as Friedrich Hayek and Milton Friedman have been affiliated with it.

National health insurance: a policy that provides health insurance for all of the citizens of a country. The first national health insurance program was implemented in Germany, followed by programs in the United Kingdom.

Naturalized British citizen: when a person from overseas becomes a British citizen after residing in the United Kingdom for five years.

Nazi: an extreme right-wing political party that ruled Germany between 1933 and 1945. The Nazis (short for National Socialists) were led by Adolf Hitler.

Neo-conservatives: a branch of American conservatism that emphasizes the importance of free-market economics and the aggressive promotion of democracy via military force. Neo-conservatives are also, generally speaking, neo-liberals.

Neo-liberal: a generally right-wing stance used in relation to politicians such as Margaret Thatcher and Ronald Reagan. Neo-liberals promote free trade, privatization, deregulation, and other moves towards economic liberalization.

New Deal: a program introduced by US President Franklin D. Roosevelt (1882–1945) involving public building works and increased government support to tackle the economic depression of the 1930s.

New Democrats: the name given to the us Democratic Party following Bill Clinton's successful 1992 presidential campaign, when it came to accept less public spending and to impose tougher demands on those receiving government support—measures previously advocated by the Republican Party.

New Labour: the name given to the British Labour Party by Tony Blair during his decade as prime minister (1997–2007). New Labour aimed to modernize the image of the party by breaking from the traditional Labour platform calling for state ownership of the means of production.

Planning: see "Central planning"—the terms are used interchangeably.

Political libertarianism: an ideology that advocates minimal state involvement and a safety net consisting only of the protection provided by law and order.

Political science: an academic discipline that studies systems of governance and political behavior.

Privatization: the process of transferring ownership of governmental assets or institutions to the private sector. An example of privatization would be outsourcing the services of the postal service to a private company.

Public choice theory: a social scientific theory developed to understand how public institutions make decisions. Public choice theory is based on the assumption that public officials are self-interested.

Republican Party (United States): one of the two main political parties of the US, along with the Democratic Party. It has become a predominantly conservative party focusing on commercial and financial interests, social conservatism, and strong armed forces, and decreasing the role of the central government.

Rule of law: the principle that society should be guided by legal institutions rather than by the interconnected decisions of individuals.

Self-interest: where individuals pursue their own interests and ambitions.

Serfdom: a medieval system in which farmers were dependent on the lord of the manor for many things, requiring his permission to move or to get married. In modern serfdom, it is the State that citizens need to obey.

Skepticism: an attitude characterized by doubt and uncertainty about the truth of something.

Social democracy: a liberal democratic system with a commitment to social reform and social justice. This is often achieved by more traditional socialist policies such as support for the welfare state and nationalization of industry and services.

Socialism: a political and economic theory that advocates a system of social organization in which the means of production and distribution are owned collectively or by the state.

Soviet Union: a communist union of states administered in the capital city of Moscow. At the end of the cold war the Soviet Union was dissolved and many states adopted capitalism.

Tariff: a tax imposed on imported goods and services. Imposing tariffs is one of the most commonly used ways of creating barriers to trade.

Tea Party movement: a political movement founded within the us Republican Party in 2009 with the aim of reducing the size of the us government.

Totalitarianism: Totalitarianism refers to rule by political dictatorship and the abolition of democracy.

War on Terror: this is the term that is commonly applied to American-led actions throughout the Middle East against non-state "terrorist" actors, including al-Qaeda. It covers the drone campaign in Pakistan, the occupation of Afghanistan, and other covert and overt operations.

Welfare state: a state in which the economic and social well-being of citizens is protected by governmental institutions, usually funded by taxes. It is based on the principles of equality of opportunity, equitable distribution of wealth, and public responsibility.

World Bank: the International Bank for Reconstruction and Development, known as the World Bank, is an organization of 188 countries, based in Washington, DC, that assists low- and middle-income countries to reduce poverty and develop their economies.

World War I: an international conflict between 1914 and 1918 centered in Europe and involving the major economic world powers of the day.

World War II: a global conflict between 1939 and 1945 that pitted the Axis Powers of Nazi Germany, Fascist Italy and Imperial Japan against the Allied nations, including Britain, the United States and the USSR.

PEOPLE MENTIONED IN THE TEXT

Norman P. Barry (1944–2008) was a British philosopher who was known as a supporter of classical liberalism and free-market ideas.

William Beveridge (1879–1963) was a British economist and social reformer who is perhaps best known for writing a report that was instrumental in the development of the British welfare state following World War II.

George H. W. Bush (b. 1924) is a retired American Republican politician who served as the 41st President of the United States.

George W. Bush (b. 1946) was the 43rd president of the United States. A Republican, he was in office from 2001 to 2009.

Winston Churchill (1874–1965) was the prime minister of the United Kingdom from 1940 to 1945 and from 1951 to 1955. He was a member of the Conservative Party.

Alistair Darling (b. 1953) is a British Labour politician who served as Chancellor of the Exchequer from 2007 to 2010.

Alexis de Tocqueville (1805–1859) was a French political thinker known for his book *Democracy in America*, which is considered a seminal analysis of American life and culture.

Herman Finer (1898–1969) was a British political scientist and Fabian Socialist (that is, an advocate of socialism through gradual legal reform).

Milton Friedman (1912–2006) was a well-known American economist who taught at the University of Chicago. He is well known as a supporter of free markets and as a key player in developing the school of thought known as monetarism.

Newt Gingrich (b. 1943) is an American politician affiliated with the Republican Party who is perhaps best known for his role in the government shutdown of 1994.

Barry Goldwater (1909–98) was an American businessman and politician who is known as the charismatic architect of the American conservative movement in the 1960s.

Václav Havel (1936–2011) was a Czech writer and politician who served as president of the Czech Republic from 1993 to 2003.

Adolf Hitler (1889–1945) was a German politician who was Chancellor of Germany from 1933 to 1945 and leader of the Nazi party. Hitler is known as one of the most destructive totalitarian rulers in history.

Thomas Jefferson (1743–1826) was an American politician who served as the third president of the United States. Jefferson was also instrumental in the founding of the country and in the drafting of the Declaration of Independence.

Lyndon Johnson (1908–73) was the 36th president of the United States. He was in office from 1963 to 1969, and is known for his Great Society program, as well as for his part in the escalation of the Vietnam War.

Dennis Kavanagh (b. 1941) is a retired professor of politics, previously at the University of Liverpool.

Arthur Koestler (1905–83) was a Hungarian British author and journalist whose book *Darkness at Noon* gained international renown as an anti-totalitarian book.

Harold Laski (1893–1950) was a professor at the London School of Economics and Political Science from 1926 to 1950 and was also the chairman of the British Labour Party from 1945 to 1946.

Harold Macmillan (1894–1986) was the Conservative prime minister of the United Kingdom from 1957 to 1963.

John Major (b. 1943) is a British politician associated with the Conservative Party who served as prime minister from 1990 to 1997.

Peter Mandelson (b. 1963) is a British Labour Party politician who is credited with being one of the people responsible for reforming the Labour Party into New Labour.

Karl Marx (1818–83) was a German philosopher whose works *Capital* and *The Communist Manifesto* form the intellectual basis for communism.

John Maynard Keynes (1886–1946) was a British economist who is regarded as the founder of "Keynesianism." This is an economic ideology that advocates that the state should fight unemployment by spending money when there is an economic crisis.

Carl Menger (1840–1921) was an Austrian economist who is considered to be the founder of the Austrian School of Economics. He is also known for his contributions to the theory of marginalism.

Benito Mussolini (1883–1945) was an Italian politician who was leader of the National Fascist Party and prime minister of Italy from 1922 to 1945.

Gunnar Myrdal (1898–1987) was a Swedish economist known for his work on the theory of money and race relations—as seen, for example, in his book *An American Dilemma: The Negro Problem and Modern Democracy*.

Barack Obama (b. 1961) is an American politician currently serving as 44th president of the United States. He is notable for being the first African American president and for the passage of the Affordable Care Act under his leadership.

George Orwell (1903–50) was a British novelist best known for his book *Nineteen Eighty-Four* and who often wrote about totalitarianism and individual freedom.

Karl Popper (1902–94) was an Austrian British philosopher known for his work on the scientific method, the nature of knowledge, and the characteristics of an open society.

Anthony Quinton (1925–2010) was a British political philosopher who contributed to the topics of metaphysics, metaphilosophy, and materialism.

John Ranelagh (b. 1947) is a British political historian of the Conservative Party.

Ronald Reagan (1911–2004) was the 40th president of the United States. He was in office from 1981 to 1989.

Lionel Robbins (1898–1984) was a British economist who was known for his ongoing debate with John Maynard Keynes and for providing a popular definition of the subject of economics.

Paul Ryan (b. 1970) is an American politician of the Republican Party who in 2012 was the Republican candidate for vice-president of the United States.

Jeffrey Sachs (b. 1954) is an American economist who currently serves as director of the Earth Institute at Columbia University, dedicated to understanding the interactions between human beings and the environment. Much of Sachs's work has focused on ending global poverty.

(Lord) Robert Skidelsky (b. 1939) is a British economic historian and life peer (i.e. a member of the upper house of Parliament, also known as the House of Lords).

Adam Smith (1723–90) was a Scottish philosopher and political economist best known for his works *The Theory of Moral Sentiments* (1759) and *An Enquiry into the Nature and Causes of the Wealth of Nations* (1776); the latter is widely considered the first modern work of economics.

Robert Solow (b. 1924) is an American economist who helped develop the theory of economic growth, specifically the Solow growth model.

Margaret Thatcher (1925–2013) was the prime minister of the United Kingdom from 1979 to 1990. Her time as prime minister was characterized by the promotion of free enterprise at the expense of governmental programs and services.

Ludwig von Mises (1881–1973) was an Austrian economist best known for his work on human choice and as one of the founding fathers of the Austrian School of Economics.

WORKS CITED

WORKS CITED

"The Coalition: Our Programme for Government." Accessed March 8, 2015. https://www.gov.uk/government/uploads/system/uploads/attachment_data/file/78977/coalition_programme_for_government.pdf.

"Friedrich August Hayek." *Library of Economics and Liberty*. Accessed March 8, 2015. http://www.econlib.org/library/Enc/bios/Hayek.html.

"Interview: Jeffrey Sachs." *Omni* 13, no. 9 (1991).

"Maestro of Economics." *The Times*, March 25, 1992.

"Mercatus Center." Accessed March 8, 2015. http://ppe.mercatus.org/.

"Sir Antony Fisher; Obituary." *The Times*, July 12, 1988.

Barry, Norman P. *Hayek's Social and Economic Philosophy*. London: Macmillan, 1979.

Beck, Glenn. "Is US Traveling Down 'Road to Serfdom'?" *Fox News*. Accessed March 6, 2015. http://www.foxnews.com/story/2010/06/09/glenn-beck-is-us-traveling-down-road-to-serfdom/.

Behrens, Robert. *The Conservative Party from Heath to Thatcher: Policies and Politics 1974–1979*. Farnborough: Saxon House, 1980.

Boettke, Peter. "Austrian School of Economics." *Library of Economics and Liberty*. Accessed March 5, 2015. http://www.econlib.org/library/Enc/AustrianSchoolofEconomics.html.

"Teaching Austrian Economics to Graduate Students." *Journal of Economics and Finance Education* 10, no. 2 (2011).

Boettke, Peter J., and Peter T. Leeson. "An 'Austrian' Perspective on Public Choice." In *Encyclopedia of Public Choice*, edited by Charles K. Rowley and Friedrich Schneider. Boston, MA: Kluwer, 2003.

Brittan, Samuel. "Hayek, Friedrich August (1899–1992)." In *Oxford Dictionary of National Biography*. Oxford: Oxford University Press, 2004.

Bush, George H. W. "Remarks on Presenting the Presidential Medal of Freedom Awards, 18 November 1991." George Bush Presidential Library and Museum. Accessed January 24, 2014. http://bushlibrary.tamu.edu/research/public_papers.php?id=3642&year=&month.

Caldwell, Bruce. *Hayek's Challenge: An Intellectual Biography of F. A. Hayek*. Chicago: University of Chicago Press, 2004.

Campbell, John. *The Grocer's Daughter*. Vol. 1 of *Margaret Thatcher*. London: Vintage, 2007.

Clarke, Peter. "*Keynes–Hayek* by Nicholas Wapshott – Review." *Guardian*, February 3, 2012. Accessed January 24, 2014. http://www.theguardian.com/books/2012/feb/03/keynes-hayek-nicholas-wapshott-review.

Cockett, Richard. *Thinking the Unthinkable: Think Tanks and the Economic Counter-Revolution, 1931–1983*. London: HarperCollins, 1994.

Crowley, Brian Lee. *The Self, the Individual, and the Community: Liberalism in the Political Thought of F. A. Hayek and Sidney and Beatrice Webb*. Oxford: Clarendon Press, 1987.

Crowley, Michael. "The Big Idea Guy." *Time Magazine*, September 3, 2012. Accessed January 24, 2014. http://www.content.time.com/time/magazine/article/0,9171,2122768,00.html.

Darling, Alistair. *Back From the Brink: 1000 Days at Number 11*. London: Atlantic Books, 2011.

Devine, C. Maury, Claudia M. Dissel, and Kim D. Parrish (Eds). *The Harvard Guide to Influential Books: 113 Distinguished Harvard Professors Discuss the Books That Have Helped to Shape Their Thinking*. New York: Harper & Row, 1986, 187.

Ebenstein, Alan. *Friedrich Hayek: A Biography*. New York: St. Martin's Press, 2001.

Edwards, Lee. *Goldwater*. Washington, DC: Regnery, 1995.

Finer, Herman. *The Road to Reaction*. Boston: Little Brown and Company, 1945.

Harris, Robin. *The Conservatives: A History*. London: Bantam, 2011.

Hart, Steve. "Equality Must Be at the Centre of a Vision for a Better Society." *New Statesman*, September 11, 2012. Accessed January 24, 2014. http://www.newstatesman.com/blogs/economics/2012/09/equality-must-be-centre-vision-better-society.

Havel, Václav. *To the Castle and Back*. London: Portobello, 2008.

Hayek, F. A. *The Counter-Revolution of Science: Studies on the Abuse of Reason*. Glencoe, IL: Free Press, 1952.

Hayek on Hayek: An Autobiographical Dialogue – The Collected Works of F. A. Hayek. Edited by Stephen Kresge and Leif Wenar. London: Routledge, 1994.

"Prize Lecture: The Pretense of Knowledge." http://www.nobelprize.org/nobel_prizes/economic-sciences/laureates/1974/hayek-lecture.html.

The Road to Serfdom – Condensed Version. Reader's Digest, 1999.

The Road to Serfdom: Texts and Documents – The Definitive Edition. Edited by Bruce Caldwell. Chicago, IL: Chicago University Press, 2007.

Hayes, Calvin. *Popper, Hayek and the Open Society*. London: Routledge, 2009.

Hickson, Kevin. "Economic Thought." In *New Labour, Old Labour: The Wilson and Callaghan Governments, 1974–79*, edited by Anthony Seldon and Kevin Hickson, 34–53. London: Routledge, 2004.

Hurt-McCarty, Marilu. *The Nobel Laureates: How the World's Greatest Economic Minds Shaped Modern Thought*. New York: McGraw-Hill, 2000.

Johnson, Paul. *Modern Times: The World from the Twenties to the Eighties*. New York: Harper & Row, 1983.

Kavanagh, Dennis. "The Making of Thatcherism: 1974–1979." In *Recovering Power: The Conservatives in Opposition since 1867*, edited by Stuart Ball and Anthony Seldon, 219–42. Basingstoke: Palgrave Macmillan, 2005.

Keynes, John Maynard. *The General Theory of Employment, Interest, and Money*. London: Macmillan, 1936.

Machlup, Fritz. *Essays on Hayek*. London: Routledge & Kegan Paul, 1977.

Macmillan, Harold. *The Middle Way*. London: Macmillan, 1938.

Marx, Karl, and Friedrich Engels. *The Communist Manifesto*. New York: Simon and Schuster, 1964.

Pethokoukis, James. "Obamacare, Meet Hayek." *American Enterprise Institute*. Accessed March 8, 2015. http://www.aei.org/publication/obamacare-meet-hayek/.

Quinton, Anthony, editor. *Political Philosophy*. Oxford: Oxford University Press, 1967.

Ranelagh, John. *Thatcher's People: An Insider's Account of the Politics, the Power and the Personalities*. London: Fontana, 1991.

Reagan, Ronald. *The Reagan Diaries*. Edited by Douglas Brinkley. New York: HarperCollins, 2007.

Robbins, Lionel. *An Essay on the Nature and Significance of Economic Science*. London: Macmillan, 1935.

Seldon, Arthur. "Friedrich von Hayek." *The Times*, March 27, 1992.

Skidelsky, Robert. "The Keynes–Hayek Rematch." Project Syndicate, August 19, 2011. Accessed January 24, 2014. http://www.project-syndicate.org/commentary/the-keynes-hayek-rematch.

Smith, Adam. *An Inquiry into the Nature and Causes of the Wealth of Nations*. London, 1799.

Smith, Vernon. "Reflections on Human Action after 50 years." *Cato Journal* 9, no. 2, Fall (1999).

Solow, Robert. "Hayek, Friedman, and the Illusions of Conservative Economics." *New Republic*. Accessed March 5, 2015. http://www.newrepublic.com/article/books-and-arts/magazine/110196/hayek-friedman-and-the-illusions-conservative-economics.

Thatcher, Margaret. *The Downing Street Years*. New York: Harper Collins, 1993, 12–13.

von Mises, Ludwig. *Socialism: An Economic and Sociological Analysis*. Auburn, AL: Ludwig von Mises Institute, 2009.

Wetterberg, Gunnar. *Pengarna & Makten: Riksbankens Historia*. Stockholm: Sveriges Riksbank i samarbete med Atlantis, 2009.

Willetts, David. "The New Conservatism? 1945–1951." In *Recovering Power: The Conservatives in Opposition since 1867*, edited by Stuart Ball and Anthony Seldon, 169–91. Basingstoke: Palgrave Macmillan, 2005.

Wootton, Barbara. *Freedom Under Planning*. Chapel Hill, NC: University of North Carolina Press, 1945.

Young, Hugo. *One of Us: A Biography of Margaret Thatcher*. London: Macmillan, 1991.

THE MACAT LIBRARY
BY DISCIPLINE

AFRICANA STUDIES

Chinua Achebe's *An Image of Africa: Racism in Conrad's Heart of Darkness*
W. E. B. Du Bois's *The Souls of Black Folk*
Zora Neale Huston's *Characteristics of Negro Expression*
Martin Luther King Jr's *Why We Can't Wait*
Toni Morrison's *Playing in the Dark: Whiteness in the American Literary Imagination*

ANTHROPOLOGY

Arjun Appadurai's *Modernity at Large: Cultural Dimensions of Globalisation*
Philippe Ariès's *Centuries of Childhood*
Franz Boas's *Race, Language and Culture*
Kim Chan & Renée Mauborgne's *Blue Ocean Strategy*
Jared Diamond's *Guns, Germs & Steel: the Fate of Human Societies*
Jared Diamond's *Collapse: How Societies Choose to Fail or Survive*
E. E. Evans-Pritchard's *Witchcraft, Oracles and Magic Among the Azande*
James Ferguson's *The Anti-Politics Machine*
Clifford Geertz's *The Interpretation of Cultures*
David Graeber's *Debt: the First 5000 Years*
Karen Ho's *Liquidated: An Ethnography of Wall Street*
Geert Hofstede's *Culture's Consequences: Comparing Values, Behaviors, Institutes and Organizations across Nations*
Claude Lévi-Strauss's *Structural Anthropology*
Jay Macleod's *Ain't No Makin' It: Aspirations and Attainment in a Low-Income Neighborhood*
Saba Mahmood's *The Politics of Piety: The Islamic Revival and the Feminist Subject*
Marcel Mauss's *The Gift*

BUSINESS

Jean Lave & Etienne Wenger's *Situated Learning*
Theodore Levitt's *Marketing Myopia*
Burton G. Malkiel's *A Random Walk Down Wall Street*
Douglas McGregor's *The Human Side of Enterprise*
Michael Porter's *Competitive Strategy: Creating and Sustaining Superior Performance*
John Kotter's *Leading Change*
C. K. Prahalad & Gary Hamel's *The Core Competence of the Corporation*

CRIMINOLOGY

Michelle Alexander's *The New Jim Crow: Mass Incarceration in the Age of Colorblindness*
Michael R. Gottfredson & Travis Hirschi's *A General Theory of Crime*
Richard Herrnstein & Charles A. Murray's *The Bell Curve: Intelligence and Class Structure in American Life*
Elizabeth Loftus's *Eyewitness Testimony*
Jay Macleod's *Ain't No Makin' It: Aspirations and Attainment in a Low-Income Neighborhood*
Philip Zimbardo's *The Lucifer Effect*

ECONOMICS

Janet Abu-Lughod's *Before European Hegemony*
Ha-Joon Chang's *Kicking Away the Ladder*
David Brion Davis's *The Problem of Slavery in the Age of Revolution*
Milton Friedman's *The Role of Monetary Policy*
Milton Friedman's *Capitalism and Freedom*
David Graeber's *Debt: the First 5000 Years*
Friedrich Hayek's *The Road to Serfdom*
Karen Ho's *Liquidated: An Ethnography of Wall Street*

John Maynard Keynes's *The General Theory of Employment, Interest and Money*
Charles P. Kindleberger's *Manias, Panics and Crashes*
Robert Lucas's *Why Doesn't Capital Flow from Rich to Poor Countries?*
Burton G. Malkiel's *A Random Walk Down Wall Street*
Thomas Robert Malthus's *An Essay on the Principle of Population*
Karl Marx's *Capital*
Thomas Piketty's *Capital in the Twenty-First Century*
Amartya Sen's *Development as Freedom*
Adam Smith's *The Wealth of Nations*
Nassim Nicholas Taleb's *The Black Swan: The Impact of the Highly Improbable*
Amos Tversky's & Daniel Kahneman's *Judgment under Uncertainty: Heuristics and Biases*
Mahbub Ul Haq's *Reflections on Human Development*
Max Weber's *The Protestant Ethic and the Spirit of Capitalism*

FEMINISM AND GENDER STUDIES

Judith Butler's *Gender Trouble*
Simone De Beauvoir's *The Second Sex*
Michel Foucault's *History of Sexuality*
Betty Friedan's *The Feminine Mystique*
Saba Mahmood's *The Politics of Piety: The Islamic Revival and the Feminist Subject*
Joan Wallach Scott's *Gender and the Politics of History*
Mary Wollstonecraft's *A Vindication of the Rights of Woman*
Virginia Woolf's *A Room of One's Own*

GEOGRAPHY

The Brundtland Report's *Our Common Future*
Rachel Carson's *Silent Spring*
Charles Darwin's *On the Origin of Species*
James Ferguson's *The Anti-Politics Machine*
Jane Jacobs's *The Death and Life of Great American Cities*
James Lovelock's *Gaia: A New Look at Life on Earth*
Amartya Sen's *Development as Freedom*
Mathis Wackernagel & William Rees's *Our Ecological Footprint*

HISTORY

Janet Abu-Lughod's *Before European Hegemony*
Benedict Anderson's *Imagined Communities*
Bernard Bailyn's *The Ideological Origins of the American Revolution*
Hanna Batatu's *The Old Social Classes And The Revolutionary Movements Of Iraq*
Christopher Browning's *Ordinary Men: Reserve Police Batallion 101 and the Final Solution in Poland*
Edmund Burke's *Reflections on the Revolution in France*
William Cronon's *Nature's Metropolis: Chicago And The Great West*
Alfred W. Crosby's *The Columbian Exchange*
Hamid Dabashi's *Iran: A People Interrupted*
David Brion Davis's *The Problem of Slavery in the Age of Revolution*
Nathalie Zemon Davis's *The Return of Martin Guerre*
Jared Diamond's *Guns, Germs & Steel: the Fate of Human Societies*
Frank Dikotter's *Mao's Great Famine*
John W Dower's *War Without Mercy: Race And Power In The Pacific War*
W. E. B. Du Bois's *The Souls of Black Folk*
Richard J. Evans's *In Defence of History*
Lucien Febvre's *The Problem of Unbelief in the 16th Century*
Sheila Fitzpatrick's *Everyday Stalinism*

Eric Foner's *Reconstruction: America's Unfinished Revolution, 1863-1877*
Michel Foucault's *Discipline and Punish*
Michel Foucault's *History of Sexuality*
Francis Fukuyama's *The End of History and the Last Man*
John Lewis Gaddis's *We Now Know: Rethinking Cold War History*
Ernest Gellner's *Nations and Nationalism*
Eugene Genovese's *Roll, Jordan, Roll: The World the Slaves Made*
Carlo Ginzburg's *The Night Battles*
Daniel Goldhagen's *Hitler's Willing Executioners*
Jack Goldstone's *Revolution and Rebellion in the Early Modern World*
Antonio Gramsci's *The Prison Notebooks*
Alexander Hamilton, John Jay & James Madison's *The Federalist Papers*
Christopher Hill's *The World Turned Upside Down*
Carole Hillenbrand's *The Crusades: Islamic Perspectives*
Thomas Hobbes's *Leviathan*
Eric Hobsbawm's *The Age Of Revolution*
John A. Hobson's *Imperialism: A Study*
Albert Hourani's *History of the Arab Peoples*
Samuel P. Huntington's *The Clash of Civilizations and the Remaking of World Order*
C. L. R. James's *The Black Jacobins*
Tony Judt's *Postwar: A History of Europe Since 1945*
Ernst Kantorowicz's *The King's Two Bodies: A Study in Medieval Political Theology*
Paul Kennedy's *The Rise and Fall of the Great Powers*
Ian Kershaw's *The "Hitler Myth": Image and Reality in the Third Reich*
John Maynard Keynes's *The General Theory of Employment, Interest and Money*
Charles P. Kindleberger's *Manias, Panics and Crashes*
Martin Luther King Jr's *Why We Can't Wait*
Henry Kissinger's *World Order: Reflections on the Character of Nations and the Course of History*
Thomas Kuhn's *The Structure of Scientific Revolutions*
Georges Lefebvre's *The Coming of the French Revolution*
John Locke's *Two Treatises of Government*
Niccolò Machiavelli's *The Prince*
Thomas Robert Malthus's *An Essay on the Principle of Population*
Mahmood Mamdani's *Citizen and Subject: Contemporary Africa And The Legacy Of Late Colonialism*
Karl Marx's *Capital*
Stanley Milgram's *Obedience to Authority*
John Stuart Mill's *On Liberty*
Thomas Paine's *Common Sense*
Thomas Paine's *Rights of Man*
Geoffrey Parker's *Global Crisis: War, Climate Change and Catastrophe in the Seventeenth Century*
Jonathan Riley-Smith's *The First Crusade and the Idea of Crusading*
Jean-Jacques Rousseau's *The Social Contract*
Joan Wallach Scott's *Gender and the Politics of History*
Theda Skocpol's *States and Social Revolutions*
Adam Smith's *The Wealth of Nations*
Timothy Snyder's *Bloodlands: Europe Between Hitler and Stalin*
Sun Tzu's *The Art of War*
Keith Thomas's *Religion and the Decline of Magic*
Thucydides's *The History of the Peloponnesian War*
Frederick Jackson Turner's *The Significance of the Frontier in American History*
Odd Arne Westad's *The Global Cold War: Third World Interventions And The Making Of Our Times*

The Macat Library By Discipline

LITERATURE

Chinua Achebe's *An Image of Africa: Racism in Conrad's Heart of Darkness*
Roland Barthes's *Mythologies*
Homi K. Bhabha's *The Location of Culture*
Judith Butler's *Gender Trouble*
Simone De Beauvoir's *The Second Sex*
Ferdinand De Saussure's *Course in General Linguistics*
T. S. Eliot's *The Sacred Wood: Essays on Poetry and Criticism*
Zora Neale Huston's *Characteristics of Negro Expression*
Toni Morrison's *Playing in the Dark: Whiteness in the American Literary Imagination*
Edward Said's *Orientalism*
Gayatri Chakravorty Spivak's *Can the Subaltern Speak?*
Mary Wollstonecraft's *A Vindication of the Rights of Women*
Virginia Woolf's *A Room of One's Own*

PHILOSOPHY

Elizabeth Anscombe's *Modern Moral Philosophy*
Hannah Arendt's *The Human Condition*
Aristotle's *Metaphysics*
Aristotle's *Nicomachean Ethics*
Edmund Gettier's *Is Justified True Belief Knowledge?*
Georg Wilhelm Friedrich Hegel's *Phenomenology of Spirit*
David Hume's *Dialogues Concerning Natural Religion*
David Hume's *The Enquiry for Human Understanding*
Immanuel Kant's *Religion within the Boundaries of Mere Reason*
Immanuel Kant's *Critique of Pure Reason*
Søren Kierkegaard's *The Sickness Unto Death*
Søren Kierkegaard's *Fear and Trembling*
C. S. Lewis's *The Abolition of Man*
Alasdair MacIntyre's *After Virtue*
Marcus Aurelius's *Meditations*
Friedrich Nietzsche's *On the Genealogy of Morality*
Friedrich Nietzsche's *Beyond Good and Evil*
Plato's *Republic*
Plato's *Symposium*
Jean-Jacques Rousseau's *The Social Contract*
Gilbert Ryle's *The Concept of Mind*
Baruch Spinoza's *Ethics*
Sun Tzu's *The Art of War*
Ludwig Wittgenstein's *Philosophical Investigations*

POLITICS

Benedict Anderson's *Imagined Communities*
Aristotle's *Politics*
Bernard Bailyn's *The Ideological Origins of the American Revolution*
Edmund Burke's *Reflections on the Revolution in France*
John C. Calhoun's *A Disquisition on Government*
Ha-Joon Chang's *Kicking Away the Ladder*
Hamid Dabashi's *Iran: A People Interrupted*
Hamid Dabashi's *Theology of Discontent: The Ideological Foundation of the Islamic Revolution in Iran*
Robert Dahl's *Democracy and its Critics*
Robert Dahl's *Who Governs?*
David Brion Davis's *The Problem of Slavery in the Age of Revolution*

Alexis De Tocqueville's *Democracy in America*
James Ferguson's *The Anti-Politics Machine*
Frank Dikotter's *Mao's Great Famine*
Sheila Fitzpatrick's *Everyday Stalinism*
Eric Foner's *Reconstruction: America's Unfinished Revolution, 1863-1877*
Milton Friedman's *Capitalism and Freedom*
Francis Fukuyama's *The End of History and the Last Man*
John Lewis Gaddis's *We Now Know: Rethinking Cold War History*
Ernest Gellner's *Nations and Nationalism*
David Graeber's *Debt: the First 5000 Years*
Antonio Gramsci's *The Prison Notebooks*
Alexander Hamilton, John Jay & James Madison's *The Federalist Papers*
Friedrich Hayek's *The Road to Serfdom*
Christopher Hill's *The World Turned Upside Down*
Thomas Hobbes's *Leviathan*
John A. Hobson's *Imperialism: A Study*
Samuel P. Huntington's *The Clash of Civilizations and the Remaking of World Order*
Tony Judt's *Postwar: A History of Europe Since 1945*
David C. Kang's *China Rising: Peace, Power and Order in East Asia*
Paul Kennedy's *The Rise and Fall of Great Powers*
Robert Keohane's *After Hegemony*
Martin Luther King Jr.'s *Why We Can't Wait*
Henry Kissinger's *World Order: Reflections on the Character of Nations and the Course of History*
John Locke's *Two Treatises of Government*
Niccolò Machiavelli's *The Prince*
Thomas Robert Malthus's *An Essay on the Principle of Population*
Mahmood Mamdani's *Citizen and Subject: Contemporary Africa And The Legacy Of Late Colonialism*
Karl Marx's *Capital*
John Stuart Mill's *On Liberty*
John Stuart Mill's *Utilitarianism*
Hans Morgenthau's *Politics Among Nations*
Thomas Paine's *Common Sense*
Thomas Paine's *Rights of Man*
Thomas Piketty's *Capital in the Twenty-First Century*
Robert D. Putman's *Bowling Alone*
John Rawls's *Theory of Justice*
Jean-Jacques Rousseau's *The Social Contract*
Theda Skocpol's *States and Social Revolutions*
Adam Smith's *The Wealth of Nations*
Sun Tzu's *The Art of War*
Henry David Thoreau's *Civil Disobedience*
Thucydides's *The History of the Peloponnesian War*
Kenneth Waltz's *Theory of International Politics*
Max Weber's *Politics as a Vocation*
Odd Arne Westad's *The Global Cold War: Third World Interventions And The Making Of Our Times*

POSTCOLONIAL STUDIES

Roland Barthes's *Mythologies*
Frantz Fanon's *Black Skin, White Masks*
Homi K. Bhabha's *The Location of Culture*
Gustavo Gutiérrez's *A Theology of Liberation*
Edward Said's *Orientalism*
Gayatri Chakravorty Spivak's *Can the Subaltern Speak?*

The Macat Library By Discipline

PSYCHOLOGY

Gordon Allport's *The Nature of Prejudice*
Alan Baddeley & Graham Hitch's *Aggression: A Social Learning Analysis*
Albert Bandura's *Aggression: A Social Learning Analysis*
Leon Festinger's *A Theory of Cognitive Dissonance*
Sigmund Freud's *The Interpretation of Dreams*
Betty Friedan's *The Feminine Mystique*
Michael R. Gottfredson & Travis Hirschi's *A General Theory of Crime*
Eric Hoffer's *The True Believer: Thoughts on the Nature of Mass Movements*
William James's *Principles of Psychology*
Elizabeth Loftus's *Eyewitness Testimony*
A. H. Maslow's *A Theory of Human Motivation*
Stanley Milgram's *Obedience to Authority*
Steven Pinker's *The Better Angels of Our Nature*
Oliver Sacks's *The Man Who Mistook His Wife For a Hat*
Richard Thaler & Cass Sunstein's *Nudge: Improving Decisions About Health, Wealth and Happiness*
Amos Tversky's *Judgment under Uncertainty: Heuristics and Biases*
Philip Zimbardo's *The Lucifer Effect*

SCIENCE

Rachel Carson's *Silent Spring*
William Cronon's *Nature's Metropolis: Chicago And The Great West*
Alfred W. Crosby's *The Columbian Exchange*
Charles Darwin's *On the Origin of Species*
Richard Dawkin's *The Selfish Gene*
Thomas Kuhn's *The Structure of Scientific Revolutions*
Geoffrey Parker's *Global Crisis: War, Climate Change and Catastrophe in the Seventeenth Century*
Mathis Wackernagel & William Rees's *Our Ecological Footprint*

SOCIOLOGY

Michelle Alexander's *The New Jim Crow: Mass Incarceration in the Age of Colorblindness*
Gordon Allport's *The Nature of Prejudice*
Albert Bandura's *Aggression: A Social Learning Analysis*
Hanna Batatu's *The Old Social Classes And The Revolutionary Movements Of Iraq*
Ha-Joon Chang's *Kicking Away the Ladder*
W. E. B. Du Bois's *The Souls of Black Folk*
Émile Durkheim's *On Suicide*
Frantz Fanon's *Black Skin, White Masks*
Frantz Fanon's *The Wretched of the Earth*
Eric Foner's *Reconstruction: America's Unfinished Revolution, 1863-1877*
Eugene Genovese's *Roll, Jordan, Roll: The World the Slaves Made*
Jack Goldstone's *Revolution and Rebellion in the Early Modern World*
Antonio Gramsci's *The Prison Notebooks*
Richard Herrnstein & Charles A Murray's *The Bell Curve: Intelligence and Class Structure in American Life*
Eric Hoffer's *The True Believer: Thoughts on the Nature of Mass Movements*
Jane Jacobs's *The Death and Life of Great American Cities*
Robert Lucas's *Why Doesn't Capital Flow from Rich to Poor Countries?*
Jay Macleod's *Ain't No Makin' It: Aspirations and Attainment in a Low Income Neighborhood*
Elaine May's *Homeward Bound: American Families in the Cold War Era*
Douglas McGregor's *The Human Side of Enterprise*
C. Wright Mills's *The Sociological Imagination*

Thomas Piketty's *Capital in the Twenty-First Century*
Robert D. Putman's *Bowling Alone*
David Riesman's *The Lonely Crowd: A Study of the Changing American Character*
Edward Said's *Orientalism*
Joan Wallach Scott's *Gender and the Politics of History*
Theda Skocpol's *States and Social Revolutions*
Max Weber's *The Protestant Ethic and the Spirit of Capitalism*

THEOLOGY

Augustine's *Confessions*
Benedict's *Rule of St Benedict*
Gustavo Gutiérrez's *A Theology of Liberation*
Carole Hillenbrand's *The Crusades: Islamic Perspectives*
David Hume's *Dialogues Concerning Natural Religion*
Immanuel Kant's *Religion within the Boundaries of Mere Reason*
Ernst Kantorowicz's *The King's Two Bodies: A Study in Medieval Political Theology*
Søren Kierkegaard's *The Sickness Unto Death*
C. S. Lewis's *The Abolition of Man*
Saba Mahmood's *The Politics of Piety: The Islamic Revival and the Feminist Subject*
Baruch Spinoza's *Ethics*
Keith Thomas's *Religion and the Decline of Magic*

COMING SOON

Chris Argyris's *The Individual and the Organisation*
Seyla Benhabib's *The Rights of Others*
Walter Benjamin's *The Work Of Art in the Age of Mechanical Reproduction*
John Berger's *Ways of Seeing*
Pierre Bourdieu's *Outline of a Theory of Practice*
Mary Douglas's *Purity and Danger*
Roland Dworkin's *Taking Rights Seriously*
James G. March's *Exploration and Exploitation in Organisational Learning*
Ikujiro Nonaka's *A Dynamic Theory of Organizational Knowledge Creation*
Griselda Pollock's *Vision and Difference*
Amartya Sen's *Inequality Re-Examined*
Susan Sontag's *On Photography*
Yasser Tabbaa's *The Transformation of Islamic Art*
Ludwig von Mises's *Theory of Money and Credit*

The Macat Library By Discipline

Macat Disciplines

Access the greatest ideas and thinkers across entire disciplines, including

INEQUALITY

Ha-Joon Chang's, *Kicking Away the Ladder*
David Graeber's, *Debt: The First 5000 Years*
Robert E. Lucas's, *Why Doesn't Capital Flow from Rich To Poor Countries?*
Thomas Piketty's, *Capital in the Twenty-First Century*
Amartya Sen's, *Inequality Re-Examined*
Mahbub Ul Haq's, *Reflections on Human Development*

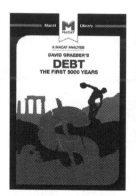

Macat analyses are available from all good bookshops and libraries.

Access hundreds of analyses through one, multimedia tool.

Join free for one month **library.macat.com**

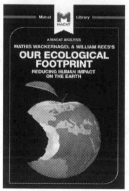

Macat Pairs

Analyse historical and modern issues from opposite sides of an argument. Pairs include:

INTERNATIONAL RELATIONS IN THE 21ˢᵀ CENTURY

Samuel P. Huntington's
The Clash of Civilisations

In his highly influential 1996 book, Huntington offers a vision of a post-Cold War world in which conflict takes place not between competing ideologies but between cultures. The worst clash, he argues, will be between the Islamic world and the West: the West's arrogance and belief that its culture is a "gift" to the world will come into conflict with Islam's obstinacy and concern that its culture is under attack from a morally decadent "other."

Clash inspired much debate between different political schools of thought. But its greatest impact came in helping define American foreign policy in the wake of the 2001 terrorist attacks in New York and Washington.

Francis Fukuyama's
The End of History and the Last Man

Published in 1992, *The End of History and the Last Man* argues that capitalist democracy is the final destination for all societies. Fukuyama believed democracy triumphed during the Cold War because it lacks the "fundamental contradictions" inherent in communism and satisfies our yearning for freedom and equality. Democracy therefore marks the endpoint in the evolution of ideology, and so the "end of history." There will still be "events," but no fundamental change in ideology.

Macat Pairs

Analyse historical and modern issues from opposite sides of an argument. Pairs include:

ARE WE FUNDAMENTALLY GOOD - OR BAD?

Steven Pinker's
The Better Angels of Our Nature

Stephen Pinker's gloriously optimistic 2011 book argues that, despite humanity's biological tendency toward violence, we are, in fact, less violent today than ever before. To prove his case, Pinker lays out pages of detailed statistical evidence. For him, much of the credit for the decline goes to the eighteenth-century Enlightenment movement, whose ideas of liberty, tolerance, and respect for the value of human life filtered down through society and affected how people thought. That psychological change led to behavioral change—and overall we became more peaceful. Critics countered that humanity could never overcome the biological urge toward violence; others argued that Pinker's statistics were flawed.

Philip Zimbardo's
The Lucifer Effect

Some psychologists believe those who commit cruelty are innately evil. Zimbardo disagrees. In *The Lucifer Effect*, he argues that sometimes good people do evil things simply because of the situations they find themselves in, citing many historical examples to illustrate his point. Zimbardo details his 1971 Stanford prison experiment, where ordinary volunteers playing guards in a mock prison rapidly became abusive. But he also describes the tortures committed by US army personnel in Iraq's Abu Ghraib prison in 2003—and how he himself testified in defence of one of those guards. committed by US army personnel in Iraq's Abu Ghraib prison in 2003—and how he himself testified in defence of one of those guards.

Macat analyses are available from all good bookshops and libraries.

Access hundreds of analyses through one, multimedia tool.

Join free for one month **library.macat.com**

Macat Pairs

Analyse historical and modern issues from opposite sides of an argument. Pairs include:

HOW WE RELATE TO EACH OTHER AND SOCIETY

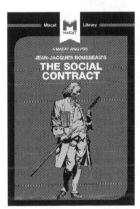

Jean-Jacques Rousseau's
The Social Contract

Rousseau's famous work sets out the radical concept of the 'social contract': a give-and-take relationship between individual freedom and social order.

If people are free to do as they like, governed only by their own sense of justice, they are also vulnerable to chaos and violence. To avoid this, Rousseau proposes, they should agree to give up some freedom to benefit from the protection of social and political organization. But this deal is only just if societies are led by the collective needs and desires of the people, and able to control the private interests of individuals. For Rousseau, the only legitimate form of government is rule by the people.

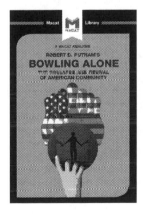

Robert D. Putnam's
Bowling Alone

In *Bowling Alone*, Robert Putnam argues that Americans have become disconnected from one another and from the institutions of their common life, and investigates the consequences of this change.

Looking at a range of indicators, from membership in formal organizations to the number of invitations being extended to informal dinner parties, Putnam demonstrates that Americans are interacting less and creating less "social capital" – with potentially disastrous implications for their society.

It would be difficult to overstate the impact of *Bowling Alone*, one of the most frequently cited social science publications of the last half-century.

Macat analyses are available from all good bookshops and libraries.

Access hundreds of analyses through one, multimedia tool.
Join free for one month **library.macat.com**

Printed in the United States
by Baker & Taylor Publisher Services